What Others Are Saying...

"In this day and age of spiritual teachers that come in every conceivable guise, *Spiritual Vampires* is an important manual on the appropriate use of power—a strategy for healthy spiritual recovery for those who have been subject to religious abuse."
—*Harvey Joyner, Jr., minister*

"This book is so timely and valuable. It will challenge our personal experiences and beliefs, and rightly so. I honor Marty for her courage to reveal these much-needed (and much-resisted) truths. The emperor truly has no clothes on!"
—*Liese Keon, MFCC, psychotherapist*

"*Vampires* was a gift sent from heaven for me! While editing this book, I had some profound personal insights related to latent incest memories that brought about a healing which allowed me to cancel a hysterectomy."
—*Colleen Rae, author of* Perchance To Dream

"Marty Raphael bravely names a form of abuse we'd rather believe does not exist. Her personal story of healing is a powerful contribution to the healing of all spiritual abuse survivors!"
—*Sandra Felt, MSW, LCSW, psychotherapist*

"I especially love the final chapters of this book because they offer hope and a vision for how it can be different. They also provide the tools necessary for preventing abuse of any sort, not only for ourselves, but for our children."
—*Karyn Wyse, minister*

"Your story (*Spiritual Vampires*) is quite moving. I am *certain* that many will find deep encouragement to return to the ever-present Truth within, and in that return to drink deeply of that which is total nourishment. Good work! Makes it *all* worth it when the story is offered up to help others."
—*Gangaji*

"The road to hell is a freeway paved with peoples' good intentions. The road from hell is a winding, unpaved path that we construct. And the end of the path is only the beginning. Oh, but what a powerful, beautiful beginning it turned out to be! Thank you for the courage to survive and to share your journey. Your book, *Spiritual Vampires,* is a gift of healing to yourself and a gift to all of us."
—*Stan Friedman, photographer and documentary producer*

"Spiritual vampirism is an insidious process. I read your book with great interest having once been a 'victim' of a so-called guru. I found some revealing answers and valuable information in the chapters dealing with how people become entangled in spiritual vampirism. Specifically the chapter on power led me to understand more clearly how my hunger for spiritual answers led me astray."
—*Sharon Holley, MS, research writer*

Spiritual Vampires

The Use and Misuse of Spiritual Power

Marty Raphael

The Message Company

Copyright © 1996 by Marty Raphael

All rights reserved. No part of this book may be used or reproduced in any manner whatsoever without the written permission of the publisher except for brief quotations embodied in critical articles, reviews, or works of scholarship.

ISBN 1-57282-006-3

Library of Congress Catalog Card Number 95-75339

First Edition

Book and cover design by Janice St. Marie
Cover illustration © 1995 by Ingrid Kelley

Cataloging in Publication Data
Raphael, Marty.
    Spiritual vampires : the use and misuse of spiritual power / Marty Raphael ; foreword by Jacquelyn small.--1st ed.
    p. cm.
    Includes bibliographical references and index.
    ISBN 1-57282-006-3

    1. Self-actualization (psychology) . 2. Raphael, Marty. 3. spiritualists-- Controversial literature. 4. Spiritual warfare. I. Title

BF637 . S4R36 1996   158. '1 B--dc20   95-75339

Published and Distributed by

The Message Company
RR2 Box 307MM
Santa Fe, New Mexico 87505
505-474-0998

Printed in the United States of America on acid-free, recycled paper

*This book is dedicated to the children,
the ones who are blessed with a burning passion for freedom.*

Contents

Acknowledgements   9
Foreword by Jacquelyn Small   11
Introduction   19

Chapter 1   **Spiritual Incest**   23
  Spirituality and Sexuality:
    Not Such Strange Bedfellows   26
  Subtle and Not So Subtle Examples of Spiritual Incest   27
  Some Serious Consequences of Spiritual Incest   36

Chapter 2   **Spiritual Vampires**   41
  Spiritual Power Defined   44
  The Difference Between Real and Fake Spiritual Power   46
  Spiritual Abuse Defined   47

Chapter 3   **Spiritual Parasites**   51

Chapter 4   **Spiritual Predators: Let Us Prey**   67

Chapter 5   **Spiritual Perpetrators**   85

Chapter 6   **The Seduction**   103
  Compulsive Religiosity   104
  The Desire to Die and the Lure of Peace   109
  Life Crisis Vulnerability   116
  Obsession with Immortality & the Fear of Death   128

Chapter 7   **Desire for Power**   141
  Learning How to Fly Without Learning How to Land   143
  Powers of the Mind   153
  Power in the Role of Martyr   163
  Power Through Affiliation with a Group   165
  Toxic Service   172

Chapter 8 **Breaking Free**	**179**
Phase 1: Recognition	181
Phase 2: Bargaining	188
Phase 3: Anger	190
Phase 4: Surrender	191
Phase 5: Grief	192
Complete Healing	193
Chapter 9 **Life without Vampires**	**203**
Spiritual Heart Attack in India	212
How is Life Different without Vampires?	215
Bali, The Last True Paradise:	
A Model for Gardening the Souls of our Children	217
Appendices	*225*
Characteristics of Spiritual Vampires	225
Characteristics of Spiritual Vampire Groups	227
Warding Off Spiritual Vampires	229
Questions to Ask When Choosing a Therapist	231
How to Pick the Good Spiritual Workshops	
and Avoid the Bad Ones	232
Directory of Resources	*235*
Bibliography	*243*
Glossary	*247*
Index	*251*

Acknowledgements

Thich Nhat Hanh, the famous Vietnamese Buddhist teacher, teaches the interconnectedness of all things. He says that no one person could ever be totally responsible for the creation of anything. And that has certainly been true in the process of creating this book. In fact, had it not been for the following people, the book would probably never have been written. The subject matter is such that I almost talked myself out of going forward with it many times.

I give thanks to John Irwin for his enthusiastic encouragement when I first conceived the idea of writing a book on spiritual abuse. Sandra Felt was most instrumental in keeping me on task when it seemed too hard to keep on keeping on. She helped me carry the vision of the book from its inception.

Laurel King also strongly encouraged me from the beginning, and, having written several books herself, was kind enough to hold the candle on the path so I could see my way. Colleen Rae, a highly skilled editor, was able to stay far enough away from the project to see the big picture and help it be formatted in a reader-friendly way. And much thanks goes to Monnie Efross and Alison Stevens for their gentle and sometimes radical editorial comments on the manuscript.

I have a special place in my heart for the spiritual abuse

survivors I interviewed, whether or not their stories made it into the book. They are the ones who have come out of denial about the problem and are carrying the burden of healing for themselves, their families, and the collective consciousness as a whole.

My partner in life and love, James Berry, is to be deeply acknowledged for his tenacious belief in me and the project. I continue to be amazed as I see more and more of his beautiful spirit and his commitment to change the world.

Foreword

Jacquelyn Small

There is an old saying I am sure we have all heard: "If you meet the Buddha on the road, kill him!" This, of course, is not a Mafia-esque mandate to murder some poor unsuspecting Indian sage. It alludes to the fact that we are never to give our power away to another human being, no matter how enlightened. We must all somehow learn—usually the hard way—that what we look up to in others as great wisdom, power, or enlightenment is really only disowned parts of our ourselves.

Because we are spiritual beings in human form, we are each responsible for coming into our own wisdom. As spiritual beings, we are not designed to ever focus for long on someone else's having come into theirs! But given the type of parenting and religious training most of us have had, it is no wonder that we have gotten so lost in others' power. Most of us travel a long journey fraught with codependency and lack of belief in ourselves before we even glimpse the fact that we are all equal beings and co-creators by divine right.

It is true, of course, that we can all learn from wise guides and true elders; we can even cherish them and model ourselves after their greatness-made-visible. But we must remember at all times that these gurus or guides, though manifested as real people in the physical world, are *internal* functions that work in our psychological lives. These functions magnetically compel us toward the realization of our own inner ideal or God-image. This intense desire to worship exists within all of our souls and imprints God's nature—which is love—upon our lives. Our will, however, belongs never to the guru, but to God. And every true spiritual teacher knows this.

Genuine spiritual guides evidence the impulses of living masters of the heart. They are willing to flow gracefully through the twists and turns of fate along *with* their students, not *over* them, as they become spiritually mature. So, no matter if their "followers" fall on their noses in abject worship of their leaders, the true teacher does not succumb to this flattery. They constantly move each student toward the recognition of his or her own strengths and self-empowerment.

My own spiritual life has always been guided from the subjective inner worlds. Since I was a child, inner guides and teachers have spoken to me from within. I was fortunate to have parents who allowed my own inner development, without ever making me feel I was wrong. Yet I, too, felt a strong pull toward four different guru paths during this life, each time driven by a vague doubt that perhaps my ego needed to be flattened into humble submission to some greater person. But each time, after a serious investigation, I came away disenchanted and unable to submit. I experienced these gurus (three males, one female) as emphatically above reproach, arrogant, and downright rude. Hardly models of compassion and spiritual truth! The starry-eyed devotees that surrounded these powerful figures, also people I did not wish to emulate, floated several feet off the ground, completely oblivious to the physical, emotional, and even in one case, sexual abuse that was blatantly obvious to any outsider. Yet, before I condemn these spiritual leaders, I must comment that it takes two to play their game. Though they are often unconscious of the fact, devotees often *plead* for what they get from their gurus—even the abuse! This is the shadow side of the devotee, and the resulting victimhood is never a solution. So the victim/perpetrator issues are alive and well on both sides of this shadow dance. The shadow, remember, is our unconscious.

Unconscious denial is a psychological disorder, and a lack of spiritual discrimination is of no service on any true spiritual path. Unconscious denial and lack of discrimination are, in fact, the key elements that empower the human shadow. When repressed, the shadow eventually acts out and wreaks havoc upon any community. This is the sacred purpose of the human shadow—to reveal to us in vivid technicolor any part of ourselves or life we are refusing to see. The more we repress our shadow and pretend we are positive only—always love and light—the bigger the shadow grows in our unconscious hidden lives. When we deny our shadow, others of our species must carry the dark side for us. Spiritual teachers, *especially*, need to remember that this is a psychological law.

Here is a truism we must never forget: *An unhealthy psyche creates a "bogus" spirituality.* Our spiritual essences must blend with good psychological health before we can live as our whole (holy) natures. Therefore, it is imperative that our egos integrate before we attempt to transcend them. Both teachers and students had best take responsibility for healing their psychological wounds and faulty egos. We must each do our own part in healing these aspects of human unconsciousness. As the great esoteric teacher Dion Fortune once humorously commented:

> *People who cannot deal with life successfully upon a single plane of existence are ill-advised to multiply their difficulties by expanding their consciousness.*

I am considered by some to be a woman who is in her power. I do not always experience myself this way, but I know this is the image that I project in my larger life as a teacher. I have many loving students I must face and work with heart to heart on a regular basis, people who look up to me as a guide or role model. Some project their ideal Mother image onto me - or their Bad Mother image when I do not measure up to their expectations. My students tell me they love me because I do not hide my flaws and the fact that I make mistakes. I receive many back-handed compliments, such as, "Jacquie, we love you because you are so human and don't mind just being yourself, shadow and all."

When I realized years ago that my shadow was so obvious to others, I was quite humiliated and felt like crawling into a hole. But later, I realized that this transparency was the gift of freedom: I was already seen for who I really was. I took note. My "on stage" and "off stage" selves began to meld into one personality years ago. And I know better than to ever appear as "having arrived." In order to survive in my role as teacher, I have had to recognize the implications of all this and take responsibility for my part in this ongoing relationship. I have learned to see the painful errors I fall into as sacred, and just as interesting as the joy and delight at the other end of the scale, when I *can* shine as "practically perfect" for a moment or two.

Once I was looking out at a group of loving people listening to me give a talk, courteously taking in every word. My heart melted: I saw that many in the audience had already come into their power as leaders themselves. Now, it was my time to stand upon a stage. They were playing student so that I could be their teacher. They were honoring me, as they had been honored themselves. What love!

No one in human form can ever be our God. Every body has a shadow tailing along behind it. The growing pains and challenges we all face, leaders and followers alike, are two sides of the same central core. Instead of remaining in so much denial of all this, we might as well admit that we all have immature, unfinished, and unconscious aspects of our natures. And often, it is in the crucible of our daily lives that the shadow is brought to light so it can be made conscious, owned, and healed. Whatever we make conscious, we have control over; whatever is left unconscious, has control over us.

In this book you are about to read, Marty Raphael tells the heartfelt story of her journey through the lessons of personal empowerment and true love—love for the real Self, of which we are all an integral part. I honor Marty's candid sharing, which helps us all be more alert to some of the darkest lessons of spiritual, sexual, and emotional abuse and come into the realization that the only authority on us lives within our own minds and hearts.

Every age brings with it a new dispensation, as some new aspect of God seeks creation: A fresh petal (quality) of the Lotus (Self) is unfolded through us to express in the world of form. God is evolving as are we! Today, at the closing of this millennium, the Piscean Age is ending, with its key quality of "devotion" to be integrated and released into the world as something we have learned how to be. We are now entering the Aquarian Age, with its keynote of "self-expression." To hang out in a state of unconscious immaturity, leaning on another to give us our truth, will no longer serve the evolving Self. Now we must learn to realize that the guru is within. And so, it stands to reason that the lessons along this line of unfolding will now be more severe.

Maybe we have gone as far as we can with pretending to be experts on others' lives, playing like we, who think of ourselves as being above others, no longer have any problems, or that we have the answers. If we are honest, we can see that we have all been in the same boat for a long, long time: hoping to find absolute truth from some enlightened "other" out there somewhere—a real master of wisdom, an advanced extraterrestrial, the one and only true path, the perfect religion or priest. The leaders of the future may not be people who try to rise above their students in some "pretend" or arrogant stance, but people who remain involved with the regular folk, living the ordinary life, knowing that we are *all* always students in this remarkable game called life.

Today, more and more people are coming into their rightful power as equal souls in human form. Yet many yearning souls are still stuck in debilitating distortions concerning issues of authentic power and true authority. Some are still unconsciously misusing their powerful positions over others, as is so evident time after time in Marty's story. And, on the other side of the equation, many are still hiding their light, afraid to come out and be seen, still so unhealed from their family-of-origin issues of abuse and neglect that they have not yet even thought of themselves as having any power potential. These folks are still looking "out there" for the absolute expert who will guarantee them the Father/Mother protection and guidance they never got as a child. This leaves them vulnerable to abuse.

In the years to come, we will each be called to heal our past and come fully into our own potent expression. This is no small feat. The full blossoming of our species-type is upon us. Just as a bud blossoms into a rose, so we are being asked to step out and show ourselves as grown-up sons and daughters of God. We do this by learning to stand tall in the light of our own souls and confidently offering our authenticity and unique talents to the world. "Unity in diversity" will be our prevailing quality of distinction, and it will unfold magnificently in a loving community of conscious souls. Perhaps our whole world will actually become this loving community of equal beings. For it is only through each of us being unflinchingly set on standing tall and doing our part in this divine scheme that we can evolve to our next place in evolution.

To once and for all balance and heal this pendulum swing of the victim/perpetrator syndrome that is staring us in the face everywhere we look, each of us must squarely face the fact that we are capable of being both the abuser and the abused. For most of us, the search has been long for the authentic spiritual life. The lessons concerning personal power come at us daily, requiring deep inner work and much courage to face ourselves and one another with total honesty, no matter what our roles. It is only those of us who have done our homework and reclaimed the disowned shadow as part of ourselves who are blessed with a sense of wholeness and a healthy spiritual life. Both the light and the dark have their rightful part to play in the realization of our whole Self. Learning to live within this tension of the opposites is perhaps the most challenging task of living in human form.

Introduction

As the daughter of a fundamentalist minister, I've had my spiritual blood sucked almost completely dry by many spiritual vampires, and I've done some vampiring myself. There's nothing more I can do to mend my past, but I can share my experience and the knowledge I've gained over the last four decades of searching for my own wholeness. My aim in this book is to raise the awareness of victims and vampires in order to radically change the way in which we spiritually support each other.

Not all ministers, therapists, workshop leaders, Twelve-Step sponsors, new age, and meditation teachers are spiritual vampires. But some are, and they're like distorted mirrors. They can't reflect the truth clearly because they are busy serving their own desperate needs for love, validation, and power. Whether ignorantly or consciously, they feed on the spiritual blood of others and become vampires. Not everyone who sits under their tutelage is vampired. It depends on the student's level of susceptibility.

This book is different than the many books written on the phenomenon of cults. It deals with much more. It names various types of spiritual abuse and describes how and why we are so susceptible. It's also different in that it is a manual on the *right* use of power. It can be a great tool for managing those wonderful spiritual powers that automatically come when we expand our consciousness.

In this book, I share my own and other spiritual abuse survivors' journeys of healing from spiritual addiction and various forms of spiritual abuse. Because these stories are true and some survivors are still being pursued by spiritual vampires, I've changed all but my own name. As you read the stories, you will begin to see what made us so susceptible to spiritual vampires. You will also learn to recognize the signs of abuse and how a person's spiritual addiction invites vampires to abuse them.

The second part of the book provides a map for healing and a vision of how it can be different so that we actually repel abuse rather than invite it in. It includes the five phases of healing that bring one back to divine groundedness or balance, plus more stories of what my own and others' spirituality looks and feels like *free* of vampires.

Please read this book with your own internal measuring stick for truth fully engaged. If it resonates for you, then I encourage you to integrate the learnings. On the other hand, I support you in screening out what doesn't fit for you. If you get nothing else out of this book, the one thing I would like to get across is that you are the one who ultimately knows best what the truth is for yourself.

*Have you ever experienced yourself
mirrored fully and without distortion?*

chapter one

Spiritual Incest

> *Our three great natural instincts, self-preservation, reproduction, and the social instinct, are the mainsprings of our lives. The force of life itself is behind them, and if their flow is thwarted, they are like a river whose channels are blocked and eventually find a leak. The devastation to those around them can be immense.*
> —Dion Fortune

AS A SMALL CHILD, I learned to fight. Most people aren't so lucky to have an obnoxious streak. But it won me my freedom. I'm going to help you win yours too.

My obnoxious streak started young. I was born in Montana, near a settlement of Sioux Indians where my parents ministered at a Nazarene church. In late June 1950, several board members had plans to take my father, who was also a carpenter, up in a small plane to get an aerial view of some land on which they intended to build a new church. He kept putting the flight off because he expected to birth me as he had all the other children and I was to be born at any time. Several weeks went by. Finally, on the morning of July 24 at 8:00 a.m., he left in the plane with two other parishioners.

At 12:05 p.m. on July 24, the town doctor birthed me. Who knows if I had anything to do with the timing of my birth, but my mother told and re-told this story with humor, remarking that I had such stubbornness and spite even as an infant that I was born on my own schedule, when my father was not around.

I was one of those children with a burning passion for freedom. I have lived with this fist in my back most of my life, and it has driven me almost over the brink a few times. The scriptures refer to it as "the hound of heaven." I am grateful for this "hound of heaven;" however, I nearly died under its brutal herding. It is only as I have gotten older that I have discovered that not everyone has this burning passion for freedom.

On my mother's side, I come from eleven generations of Christian preachers, evangelists, and ministers. The genealogy on my father's side also includes at least three generations of ministers. When I was growing up, this could have taken a greater toll had I not been so ornery. I developed some pretty interesting coping behaviors to make space for this burning passion when everyone around me seemed to want to extinguish every spark of it. I tried to look ugly as a child, was belligerent, angry, and generally mean. My mother used to say, "Martha, why does it have to be so difficult for you? Why can't it be easier like it is for the others?" She was right. It always seemed harder for me than it was for my five sisters and two brothers.

I have come to understand that I was not the problem. My environment was the problem. Many people in my community did everything in their power to break my will, destroy my creativity, and annihilate any sense I had of myself in order to control me. This is what I have come to call spiritual abuse. In this chapter I describe one aspect of spiritual abuse—spiritual incest—and the way it affected me as a child.

Spiritual incest is a term we don't hear very often. It is just now coming into our collective awareness. But I lived with it most of my life. We all know what incest is: it is one member of the family violating another family member's sexual boundaries. Since sexuality is a part of spirituality, incest qualifies as spiritual abuse too. This book, however, deals specifically with *spiritual* incest. Spiritual incest is also a violation of another's boundaries, but the boundaries that are violated go far beyond the sexual or physical. Spiritual incest involves any behavior on the part of someone who is in a position of authority that is destructive to another's spiritual development and through which a sacred trust is betrayed. Thomas Paine understood the ramifications of spiritual incest when he said:

> *Of all the tyrannies that affect mankind, tyranny in religion is the worst; every other species of tyranny is limited to the world we live in;*

but this attempts to stride beyond the grave, and seeks to pursue us into eternity.

More often than not, sexuality is involved in spiritual incest. In Peter Jenning's documentary "The Naked Truth," a cardinal from Notre Dame comments, "We've spent over $350,000,000 in the United States alone on pedophile suits. This is only the tip of the iceberg. There's no end in sight. The Catholic church may be sued out of existence."

Spirituality and Sexuality: Not Such Strange Bedfellows

Why are sexuality and spirituality not such strange bedfellows? As a species, we are pretty ignorant about sexual energy. For the most part, we seek sexual activity out of a need for a feeling of exhilaration. Like drug addicts going for the "high," we see sex as a way to get a fix. The moment of orgasm is the same as the feeling of oneness we get from a spiritual peak experience. Thinking cannot occur at the moment of orgasm. It is a moment of no mind; therefore, it is a moment of bliss. We are also blissful when we sleep. I am not speaking of the dream state. In deep sleep, there is also no thinking, so we are in bliss. It is only when we are not thinking that our bodies can physically regenerate themselves. This is why we crave sleep. This is also why we crave sex. They are both moments of no mind, bliss, regeneration. This is the same state as when we really wake up and attain enlightenment.

Subtle and Not So Subtle Examples of Spiritual Incest

I have had firsthand experience with spiritual incest of a sexual nature. One memory that is especially profound illustrates how my anger kept me alive:

The white ruffled curtains blew out the open window as my father and I sat on the wooden rocking chair. A buffet stood against one wall. My mother was out. My father had told me something with the word "God" in it that had convinced me to stay on his lap even though what he was doing with his finger to my genitals was hurting. When my sister and brother entered the room, he threw me off his lap like a dirty rag. After this incident, I went down the back steps of the house and wrote with my finger in the sand. I had not yet learned to read or write, but in my mind, I was writing a vow, and the symbol I scratched in the sand that day was as meaningful as any English word. I vowed with all my might that I would never believe anything he ever told me again. And I didn't. I not only didn't believe him, but I didn't believe anyone in that church or any other church that he pastored after that.

In the course of my healing from this molestation, I have attempted through many different therapy mediums, unsuccessfully, to discover what it was that my father said to me. Perhaps I will never know, but because he betrayed my trust, the incident qualified as spiritual incest.

This was my first scrape with a spiritual vampire and the beginning of what would be fifteen tumultuous years of sparring with my family and the church. It was the first call from my hound of heaven, which gave birth to my strong dissenting spirit and sparked my burning passion for freedom.

In retrospect, I am grateful for the strong dissenting spirit I developed. As a result of it, I know that my spirituality is authentic. It is no one else's imposed idea of spirituality. But the price I paid for this certainty was very high. I don't think such a high price needs to be paid for a child to have an authentic spiritual experience, truly her own.

Adults also suffer from spiritual incest. Prior to my birth, my mother did not want any more children, but my father had a belief that birth control of any sort was a sin. He considered it to be resistance to God's will. This was a form of spiritual incest and a misuse of spiritual power. Of course, my father was doing what he thought was right. This would not have been a problem except that the consequences of his beliefs were *forced* on someone else. What was difficult for me to forgive was the imposition of his spiritual beliefs on his wife, children, and parishioners.

Of course, having an unwanted child is another form of spiritual incest. No child should be brought into this world who is not wanted. Life is difficult enough as it is without being unwanted. With an unwanted child, neglect, which is also a betrayal of trust, is almost inevitable, as it was in my family.

Sometimes spiritual incest events leave a different sort of trail—often one that manifests somatically rather than cognitively. When I was thirty-five years old, I began having what I termed "spells." These "spells" would begin with a very thick feeling in my tongue and mouth. My saliva would increase at such a rate that I would have to periodically spit for several hours. The saliva tasted bad. I tried to drink spicy teas to relieve the slimy taste. Eventually, the symptoms would cease. After several of these "spells," my therapist and I realized memories were surfacing, and we began to focus on them. Upon focusing, the memories manifested as much more severe symptoms, such as an acute strep throat that lasted for several days. Often, while I was still in my therapist's office, I would have the feeling that the top of my head was going to burst off. With my therapist's guidance, I was able to visualize the top of my head coming off and see a toxic substance oozing out. After a few sessions of doing this, I began to get some relief from the physical symptoms of these horrific memories. It was only when I began to *accept* the body memories as valid that I found relief from the physical symptoms. This was an important realization. As long as I resisted the memories in fear of the physical discomfort that usually accompanied them or the subconscious fear of being killed for speaking about them, I could not find relief from the physical symptoms.

I have compassion for my father at this point in my life. I have come to recognize that he was himself a victim of child abuse and spiritual vampires. His inability to father me properly was due in large part to his own arrested development. Having been vampired himself, he was depleted of his own vitality; he became a psychic vacuum, absorbing energy from anyone he came across in order to refill his depleted resources just like a vampire.

How alarming it must have been for my father to find

himself behaving in a way for which he had total disgust and disrespect! When I wrote to him in August 1990, confronting him directly about the incest, he responded by letter saying, "There is no reason to bring up the past." In other words, he was saying, "Don't make me look there. It's too scary!"

Spiritual vampires are not bad. It is their behavior that is destructive. I have chosen to use the strong term *vampire* to point to the red (blood) flag of their destructive behavior. Usually, their own development has been arrested due to abuse of some kind that was done to them. They have simply lost a piece of their own spiritual development along the way and are doing the best they can with the knowledge and awareness they have. We just have to be careful not to get "sucked in" or "sucked on" by them and become vampires ourselves.

Incest survivors, or trauma survivors of any kind, commonly somatize the challenging experiences of their lives. For survivors, changes, transitions, and big leaps of growth are often expressed in physical illnesses or psychological dysfunctions of some sort. For myself, the strange thing is that my physical illnesses seemed to come *before* my transformations rather than after them. As I look back on my life, I can see how all the major illnesses of my life have been heralds of coming transformational shifts. They were signs of times to strengthen myself in preparation for the coming transformations.

I was five when my mother somehow contracted contagious hepatitis. She probably picked it up in someone's home. Every Saturday morning without fail, my mother and father made their weekly pastoral "calls." An illness in a family or an invitation to attend church the following Sunday were reason enough to warrant a visit by the pastor and his wife.

My mother was ill with hepatitis for many months. I came down with it as well. It was at this time that my mother taught me to lie very still. . ."so still," she said, "that you become the room and the pain goes away." She was unknowingly teaching me meditation. But meditation was a bad word in our family. It was what "those atheist Buddhists" did. Travailing in prayer was more our style. We did not understand the power of meditation. It was considered too passive.

As I lay still for what seemed like years—but was only three or four weeks—I realized how much hatred I had for everyone. I knew I should love everyone—that this was the sign of a holy person, like Jesus. I did love Jesus and purposed deeply in my heart to be just like him. This was the one thing that kept me looped into the church so strongly during all of my growing-up years. At this time, I prayed to Jesus to help me know the truth and be able to love others. This was a spiritual transition. Shortly after the hepatitis, I had an opportunity to test my internal measuring stick of truth in a nonsexual incident of spiritual incest with my Sunday School teacher.

I was six years old, and we were pastoring a church in Oxford, Indiana. One cold and snowy Sunday, I raised my hand in Sunday school class and declared that Jesus must have been very "mad" when he kicked the money changers out of the temple. The teacher insisted that Jesus would never get mad. But we were coloring a picture in which coins were flying in every direction. Jesus was actually kicking a table over with his foot. She claimed that Jesus was "righteously indignant." I did not know what that meant. I continued to argue with her and eventually told her she was stupid. She called me a belligerent and rude little girl and told me to "go home." When I would not go, she took me by the collar of my dress and shoved me toward the coat rack, ordering me to put my coat on and go.

I refused to put my coat on, and I refused to go home even though the parsonage was only about fifty yards away. I was so angry at her! I planted myself down on the ground between the church and the parsonage. We had missionaries visiting that day from Africa and my parents were keen on saving face, so they did not punish me when I refused to go inside for lunch. I told my mother I was going to sit there until I knew everything. I was so angry that I could not trust anyone to validate what I knew the truth to be!

That same Sunday school teacher had already asked me not to hold my hand up in response to her questions so that the other children would have a chance to answer. I hated her. And I was very concerned about the hatred I felt. I believed it was spiritually dangerous. I carried the guilt of that hatred in my heart for years. I lived daily with the supernatural threats of God's anger and hell from the church and my father. I had chronic nightmares.

When a Sunday school teacher intentionally humiliates a child, spiritual incest occurs. A Sunday school teacher is in a position of authority. The child is acculturated to trust a Sunday School teacher. Humiliation by a spiritual helper is especially damaging because a trust has been broken and something in the child dies. It messes with the child's cosmology.

That innermost place where our view of God or consciousness exists, is a place that needs utmost protection from the trespassing of others. The process of coming to our own cosmology is a critical stage in our development. It figures into the way we relate to everyone else on the planet. It figures into the way we present ourselves in the world. It figures into our feelings of security and belonging on Earth. It is very precious. It is a critical piece in the psychospiritual and emotional machinery of our beings.

I can see now that my belligerent behavior was wise in its own right. I needed to stay as independent of that narrow, oppressive, and abusive system of beliefs as possible. Conflict and drama of all kinds were effective means of warding off anyone who would not otherwise honor my boundaries. It was unfortunate there had to be so much drama in order for me to maintain my spiritual autonomy. It should not have been so difficult to freely honor and express my own, very natural spiritual development.

This is not to say that I don't bless my path. It has given me many gifts. For example, when I was six months old, I had whooping cough so badly that my mother would turn me upside down and pound my back to jar the congestion so that I could breathe. The memory of being turned upside down has never left me. To this day, the disorientation of "upside down" continues to be useful to me for dislodging congested thoughts. That was a small gift. A bigger one was the first "heralding" of a spiritual transformation, because it was after this serious bout with whooping cough that I was left for the first time with the Sioux Indians.

My mother never breast-fed any of her eight children due to the fact that she was burned from her waist up to her neck when she was eleven years old. She and my aunt were playing "house" in their basement. My mother was playing the role of "husband." They had two furnaces, one for coal and one for oil. She picked up the coal and threw it into the oil furnace and it blew up on her. She was in the hospital for one year. Her three brothers donated some of their skin for grafts on her body. As an adult, my mother continued to be terrified of fire until she died.

I was left with the Sioux Indians for periods of time during the first four years of my life while my parents went to revivals and camp meetings as evangelistic music ministers. During the times I was left on the Reservation, I was wet-nursed by several Sioux women. As a result of not having the opportunity to be nurtured at my own mother's breast, this intimate exposure to the Sioux had a deep spiritual impact on my world. I was influenced daily by the spiritual medicine of the Sioux through the natural infant bonding of breast-feeding. Of course, I did not know it then, but I see now why I could never make Christianity fit for me as it was taught in our home. It was far too narrow a worldview after the osmosis of the rich Sioux spirit.

I have never heard my older sisters or brothers speak of the Sioux in terms of transformational experiences. However, they too had daily contact with them during those years. But I do not believe their exposure to the Sioux was as intimate. In any event, my siblings have not discussed their inward journeys much with each other. Our upbringing was so one-dimensional and moralistic that the possibility of being judged as "doing it wrong" has always been too great. This lack of acceptance for diverse ideas has contributed greatly to the fact that none of us have shared our lives with each other as adults. This has been one of the greatest losses in my life.

When I was five years old, we moved to Nashville, Indiana. I remember feeling the deepest grief I had ever felt, bar none. I wondered if life was going to include more experiences of that feeling of being torn in two. At the time, I did not understand this grief. I had watched other children leave their friends and they did not seem to feel nearly as badly as I did. I now understand that I was leaving the people who were my mother, father, sisters, and brothers—the Sioux. I used to gaze at the photos in our albums of the Sioux in their full regalia, dancing and storytelling around big fires.

What I came to understand as an adult was that I was also leaving one culture for another. A very disturbing incident at age five happened to me at a camp meeting in Noggin, Indiana. I went up to a woman who was breast-feeding her baby. I hung around waiting for her to invite me to suckle as the Sioux had always done. She recoiled in disgust and horror as she got up and left. I was devastated. I carried the shame of that incident for decades. I realized much later that the woman and I were coming from two different worlds—she from the puritanical Christian world that viewed the body as a necessary evil, and I from the Sioux world of big-breasted women who invited the children to suckle them.

My parents embodied their Christian worldview daily. They often spoke of their "missionary" service to the Indians. Today, this is almost comical to me. So many of us have benefitted deeply from Native American wisdom. It would have been nice if there had been a mutual exchange—a sharing of ideas, rituals and spiritual revelations between the two traditions. But inherent in the belief system of my family's church was the belief that theirs was the only way. So, unfortunately, there was no opening for a mutual exchange of any kind. (Note: "Only way" language is a sure sign of a cult.)

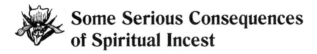 Some Serious Consequences of Spiritual Incest

There have been many other serious consequences of the spiritual and physical incest I have endured. Following are some I can point to.

- **Loss of voice.** I have struggled most of my adult life to have a voice. I sang Betsy Rose's song "Silence," about five years ago in a performance art piece I did while studying with Corey Fischer of The Traveling Jewish Theater. This song perfectly describes the confusion and paralyzation of my seized-up throat. A seized-up throat is a difficult thing for anyone, but it is much more difficult for someone who sings professionally, like myself.

- **Shame—tons of it.** I have experienced massive humiliation of my body, my sexuality, my looks, my level of intelligence, and on and on.
- **Emotional imbalance.** I have been an emotional cripple for most of my life. Out of a desperate need to feel safe, I have often not been able to recognize love or be open to it. I have also been generally contracted emotionally—afraid to open up and express myself.
- **Adrenalin addiction.** I probably developed an addiction to the adrenalin inside my own body before I was even verbal, since that was when the oral incest occurred. Later, in my adult years, I became a workaholic to the point of serious illness.
- **Relationship addiction.** Relationships for me have repeatedly involved my being loved and left. Like a broken record, this pattern has played the groove bare in my life. Early in my life, the intrinsic quality of trust that we are all naturally born with was blown out of the water for me. Trust had to be learned all over again—just as a stroke victim has to learn to talk again.
- **Learning disabilities.** If I could not trust, how could I be open to learning from others? I used to be abrasive in my questioning of everything to the point of alienating everyone who was trying to teach me anything.
- **Depression.** I battled debilitating depression of the suicidal flavor. I rarely felt like I was really living life. I always felt like I was doing time. Every day there was a feeling of, "Why am I here? When can I go?"
- **Fatigue.** Most of my life I have struggled to be

minimally functional. As I have healed, the return of my energy (chi) has definitely been one of the biggest gifts.

- **Eating Disorders.** When I was a junior in high school, I became anorexic, lost twenty-five pounds, and began having severe colitis attacks. When I was intensely emotional, my appetite would disappear. I thought that if I ate, I would lose the edge on my hypervigilence of danger. Even when I experienced a state of emotional equanimity, I would gag on food when I had to eat alone. At these times, it either tasted like human feces or dried-out cardboard.
- **Chronic back pain.** I have had chronic pain in my upper, middle, and lower back.
- **Spiritual addiction.** When I was told that I had demons hanging around me, as my family told me, I felt so badly about myself that I lost confidence in my own perceptions or views of things. I rarely had the confidence to follow my own inner guidance. I looked compulsively outside myself for answers.

The above list contains some of the "demons" I have learned to dance with in order to be functional on a daily basis. By this I mean that I have learned coping mechanisms that take into account these handicaps. This is why, when I hear discussions in support of the faulty memory syndrome, I am immediately suspicious of the people arguing for it. I suspect they are in denial of their own abusive past, or are covering up for their own vampirism, or both. It is practically impossible for me to believe that people who claim to have been incested would be making it up. There is just too much suffering related to incest. Their details may not be 100% percent accurate. But regardless, there is no doubt that something horribly traumatic happened to them.

Silence
by Betsy Rose

Silence pours into me
Like a cataract of wine reddening the sea.
And I'm drowning in a drunken melody
Which is still; which is still.

Silence breaks over me like an avalanche
Of snow burying the trees.
And I'm dreaming of a frozen melody
Which is white; which is white.

This wine of silence,
It is so sweet.
And I fear
That it will never end.

And if I do not speak,
I will die.
And if I speak,
This silence, which has become my breath
Will disappear.

chapter two

Spiritual Vampires

Spiritual Vampires
They just kept coming! They just kept coming around!
I was so tired of fighting them. I had a bone-marrow
   exhaustion.
They'd come flying in my face breathing heavy
And snorting a putrid yellow and red fire.
Some days they'd come green; hissing, slithering, leaving
Wet pussy lines in the dirt in their wake.
I never knew when they were coming. But they always came!

Sometimes when they came, they looked like God.
And I never knew it was them
Until after they'd left and I had to clean up the mess.
Sometimes they looked like the devil.
The only thing they could get from me then was my fear.
But my fear was their lunch.
I couldn't figure out what they wanted. They just kept
   coming around
As if there was no one else on the planet to taunt.

One day I realized I was so tired I couldn't stand up any longer.
So I lay down. I woke up later to find
That someone had taken me for dead and buried me out of respect.
When I awakened, sure enough, they'd come again.
That time they were primitive warrior clowns
Painted brown and orange striped.
They couldn't see me but I could see them looking nervously about.
I just lay still feeling the cool soil against my skin.
It felt as if some rotund Hawaiian mama had her arms
Around me hugging me protectively to her massive bosom.

I knew I couldn't last long with so little air.
I sung myself back to sleep after they left. I felt safe and quiet.
I must have slept that whole year, or maybe it was only forty nights.
Because when I climbed out,
I had a completely different idea about things.
I guess you could say it was a feeling.
I waited and waited expecting black blood to run down the
Pearl blue sky any minute like it used to when they were coming.
But it never happened. Nothing ever again happened like that.
So I got up and left.

I try not to look back too much.
I can't see very well in that direction.
But I met Jerupalus on the Mariposa latitude.
She laid out a grand banquet on the universal marble table.

When we'd eaten till we were completely satisfied and the food was cleared away,
She showed me how the marble table top was a map of the world.
She showed me all the places I'd been and all the places we could go.
I wasn't so interested in the places I'd been.
But I was interested in the places we could go.
So, when you get tired of dancing with the vampires
And you finally lie down,
I'll be happy to bury you, if you like.

 I HAVE KNOWN many spiritual vampires in my time. In fact, I have done some vampiring myself. In coming to an awareness of the vampiring process, I have discovered that there are three basic types of vampires: the parasite, the predator, and the perpetrator. Vampirism is a progressive disease that begins with parasitic activity, devolves to predatorial activity and finally erupts into some type of serious perpetration.

I do not believe anyone is born a vampire. We are all born filled to the brim with truth. Our spiritual journey is a process of discovering the truth that lives inside us. The way we ordinarily discover this truth is through the mirroring we get from our spiritual teachers, helpers, therapists, and so on. We all long for an undistorted mirror of the truth. And there are many mirrors. But unfortunately, there are not many mirrors that reflect the truth without distortion. Who are the vampires? They are the spiritual teachers who are distorted mirrors. They can't reflect the truth clearly because they are busy serving their own selfish and desperate needs for love, validation, and power. Whether ignorantly or consciously, they feed on the spiritual blood of others, and they are vampires. Not everyone who sits under their tutelage is vampired. Whether or not vampiring occurs depends on a student's level of susceptibility to vampires. Unfortunately, when children are the victims of vampires, they are often bled far beyond any possibility of recovery. These children grow up to be vampires themselves.

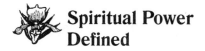 Spiritual Power Defined

Our spiritual blood is our spiritual power, which is consciousness itself. And consciousness cannot be defined. Since consciousness can not be defined, neither can spiritual power. It is tricky to talk about spiritual power or consciousness as if it were something separate from who we truly are. For example, it's dangerous to say that consciousness is "in" us. Because then we miss the important fact that the "in" is itself also consciousness. Our language speaks statically about something so dynamic that it cannot even begin to be defined. Nonetheless, for the purposes of this book, I will use the following definition of spiritual power and talk about some aspects of it.

Spiritual power is the life juice that animates human

beings. The Chinese refer to it as "chi." East Indians refer to it as "prana," the universal energy, the basic essence and source of all life. In the West, we refer to one aspect of spiritual power as the aura, which can sometimes be seen as light surrounding a holy person. This energy is inherent in all of us by virtue of the fact that we are humans. It is our Godness, our Goddessness, and our goodness—our life force.

One way we can get a feel for our life juice is to think about those times when we knew someone was staring at us. We felt them staring at us even when they were behind us or outside of our range of sight. How did we know? NASA research physicist, Barbara Brennan, in her book *Hands of Light*, says this type of phenomenon occurs because of the HEF, or human energy field. In their research on the HEF, Barbara and her colleagues, Dr. Richard Dobrin and Dr. John Pierrakos, discovered that adult rage shocks a child's system like a physical shock, while grief and depression swamp it like a fog. This kind of abuse is akin to what spiritual vampires do to our human energy field. However, spiritual vampires suck out something more important than our red lifeblood. They steal our chi, our spiritual blood, our life force. Without our essential life force, our physical blood is of no use.

There was a story in the Bible that was especially interesting to me as a child. It illustrates the phenomenon of the HEF. I didn't know why I was so fascinated by it when I was a child, but now I understand that it was a confirmation of my own hypervigilence and feelings of repulsion around certain people. Jesus was in an enormous crowd of people when he turned to his disciples and asked, "Who touched me?" His disciples looked at him like he was crazy. "What do you mean, who touched you, Master? There are many people in this crowd. Many people are touching you." Jesus insisted, "No, someone has touched me. I felt energy go out." A woman who was very afraid to admit it said, "Master, I have only touched the hem of your garment. I have a long-standing issuance of blood and I hoped to be healed." Jesus looked at her compassionately and said, "You are healed this day. Your faith has made you whole."

I will never forget when I first recognized my own human energy field and life force. I recognized it after a near-death experience, which I discuss at length later in the book. I realized that I would not be able to walk or breathe if I did not have this essential life force or goodness in me. I had always thought I was essentially bad up to that time. After the near-death incident, I really "got it" that it was arrogant of me to think that I could even exist without this essential goodness. Any of us can be unaware of it, but none of us can exist without it. It is our life force, our spiritual power.

The Difference Between Real and Fake Power

The distinction between real spiritual power and fake spiritual power is that with fake spiritual power, spiritual abuse occurs. Fake spiritual power is superficial power and comes strictly from a person's ego or mental process. It is power that is exerted *over* others. "Over" is the key word. True spiritual power has an intrinsic quality. It emanates outward from a person's inner authority; it is not exerted over another person. The authentic and truly powerful person is not interested in power *over* but rather is concerned only in experiencing power *with* another person or group. He or she wisely understands that it is only when everyone wins that anyone wins.

Spiritual abuse can occur whether the one doing the "power-over" trip is in a position of authority or not. For spiritual incest to occur, however, the abuse must be done by someone in a position of authority. Otherwise, it is not technically spiritual incest. As with familial incest, a trust must be betrayed.

Spiritual vampires are the ones who take advantage of situations that allow them to have power over others. They tend to seek positions of authority and then misuse their authority to syphon off the spiritual blood (life force) of others.

Spiritual Abuse Defined

Spiritual abuse includes any malice of thought, act, or emotion that emanates from one being and is aimed at another. All spiritual abuse is a penetration of another person's human energy field. In addition, spiritual incest sometimes includes the sexual violation of a person. However, spiritual incest is not limited to the abuse of sexual energy. Our body, our sexuality, and our personality are all aspects of our spirituality. Therefore, incest, molestation, and sexual harassment as they are traditionally defined in our culture are all types of spiritual abuse.

In the myths of vampires, the victims either die or become vampires, depending on how strong they are physically. If they are relatively healthy, they can withstand death and become immortal beings with super human powers. If they are weak, they die. Victims are usually attacked while they are sleeping. Unaware that anything has changed, they are appalled at their behavior the next day. They seem to be possessed, helpless to refrain from vampiring others.

Spiritual sexual perpetrators and vampires are often similarly surprised to discover they have been attacked and equally mystified the first time they victimize others. Many purely intentioned, spiritual service workers are unknowingly made into vampires. For example, the church, through its ignorant translation of the doctrine of celibacy, makes sexual perpetrators out of many spiritual helpers. Their sexual energy is repressed for so long that its final, explosive expression is overwhelming and harmful not only to their victims, but also to themselves.

The first type of spiritual vampire is the spiritual parasite. The spiritual parasites are the ones who are not conscious of their vampiring. They vampire simply because it was also done to them. Frequently, due to compulsive subconscious repetition, spiritual parasites find themselves in careers that are natural set ups for them, for example, teaching, counseling, or any other service-related activity. They then vampire others in the same way vampiring was done to them. The dysfunctional family is a type of spiritual parasite in that each of the family members agrees to be less than whole in order to participate in the family dance.

The Second type of spiritual vampiring is the predator. Spiritual predators are spiritual workers who understand how people give their power away to them. But they do nothing to prevent it because they secretly enjoy the status and validation of having power over others. One therapist told me outright that this goes on all the time in his practice. I asked him why he allowed the unconscious abdication of power to continue in his clients. He said that he saw this phenomenon as a psychic food chain. The people on the lower levels of the psychic food chain automatically give the more highly evolved beings their power. He said, "They don't consciously do it, but they don't mind either because that's the way it's always been." What happened to the idea that therapists are trained and dedicated to support people's empowerment?

The third type of spiritual vampire is the perpetrator. Spiritual perpetrators' internal lives are such moral wastelands that, in order to maintain spiritual lives at all, they actively seek out victims for spiritual blood. They have no concern about the effect this has on their victims' souls. They are usually charming, charismatic, and cunning. They are soul murderers.

chapter three

Spiritual Parasites

Holy Brimstone
A little girl
All soft and round with long golden hair,
So curious about life and very bright!
Painfully curious about everything.

Not only about life,
But about grown-up people.
What can please them? Anything?
So grim and straight-mouthed they are!

They don't seem to notice the way the air smells
Or the soft blue of the sky
Which sometimes turns into turquoise
When you're not looking.

Or maybe it's just that they can't see the color turquoise?
Or maybe it's all only in her imagination.
When he reads that book—the big black one with the red words—
She forgets about everything nice.

He reads those words out loud sometimes:
Lakes of burning fire and brimstone. Brimstone?
She thought it must be some kind of rock that keeps hell hot.
Hell must be kept very hot!

Otherwise, everyone might want to visit there
And there would be nothing
To keep everyone good and holy,
Only the fear of that very hot place.

Holy must mean being very still, the way he is
When he reads those red words in that big black book
Without smiling
By the window, in that chair.

THE SPIRITUAL PARASITE is the most subtle of the three types of vampires. In fact, a common parasitic act that most everyone can relate to occurs when we as parents try to live out our unrealized dreams through our children. Maybe we ourselves were the children that our parents lived their own dreams through? Many people's lives are ruined this way. They can never quite discover their true passions or livelihoods after years of being pushed into careers to fulfill their parents' unlived dreams.

Another common parasitic act occurs when adults see delightfully beautiful children and want to interact with them whether or not the children are willing. I have seen many adults force themselves on children by picking them up even though the children are loudly protesting. The children may have sour facial expressions or be screaming or even kicking in protest. Adults who force themselves on children in this way are attempting to get "hits" of the children's life force. They feed on the children's natural freshness, loyalty, vulnerability, and naivete. There is a leakage of vitality, and the dominant people, the adults, are more or less consciously lapping it up, if not actually sucking it out. The children register this "leaking" on some level and this is why they protest so loudly. A temporary separation of the parties involved will clear up any parasitic vampiring that may be going on.

When I was a child, this happened to me far too frequently with evangelists, missionaries, and church people who were visiting our home. Out of a desperate need to cope with the painful physical touch of others after being sexually molested as a child, I developed a skill. I became the monkey in our family. I imitated everyone who visited our home—ministers, missionaries, and so on. My family gave me the credit and distinction of being the one who could imitate our visitors the best. This talent was useful for keeping people away. When people approached me by stroking my hair or picking me up for their own entertainment, I would imitate them by making faces in mockery of their own. I would repeat what they said in a voice as similar to theirs as I could affect. Because it was always a shock to see such a small girl imitate them, it was a successful means to put them off. I wanted to be left alone! I was hypervigilant about sexual energy, and I trusted no one. However, I liked the laughs from my family when I imitated people after they had gone. Those were some of the few times I felt included.

Another example of parasitic vampiring is the Pope's insistence that birth control methods be avoided because they are sinful. From where I sit, this sure looks like an economic issue for the Catholic church. The belief that birth control is sinful serves the Catholic church well, for there end up being a lot more Catholics to support the church financially. I honor individuals who come to their own truth about contraceptives. But when the Catholic church *imposes* this belief on people, it is contributing to the vast and horrible ramifications of overpopulation and, in many cases, the spread of AIDS. This particular dogma, which can bring with it the death of its followers, is in the same category as the Jim Jones mass murder in Guyana. Unlike the Jones incident, it creates slow death, the way a parasite in nature gradually kills a tree. Death of this kind is so subtle and gradual that it is rarely noticed as having been caused by church doctrine.

The Catholic church's ritual of confession is another way in which parasitic vampiring often takes place. The actual ritual itself is quite useful and beautiful in that it relieves the confessor's guilt for having done something he or she believes is wrong. The problem is that confession, more often than not, is used in the same way a bulemic abuses food. The bulemic eats food and then throws it up. The Catholic does the "sin" and then confesses it up. He or she does it again and confesses again, and on and on. The church gets their continued financial support (guilt money) and the confessor goes away thinking he or she is dependent on the church for their own personal integrity. This person has given their power away to the church.

The following story portrays a spiritual parasite. My doctor, who is also a good friend, asked me about something that had happened to him. He is typically poised and in control, but when he was telling me what had occurred, he looked confused and amazed. "Marty," he said, "I don't know why I had to make contact with him. It was one of those things that just happen. You know, when your eyes light on someone as if you're zapped or some such thing. It's hard to explain. I feel embarrassed telling you what happened."

Jon proceeded to tell me that the previous Saturday he had seen a stockinged but shoeless traveller in downtown Santa Fe. The man was wearing purple shorts. It was the stockinged shoelessness of the man that raised his curiosity. The first time he saw him, he brushed him from his mind and went about his errands.

But the next day, Jon saw the man on the same street again. The pavement was about 110 degrees Fahrenheit. Jon knew that socks could not protect the man's feet from that kind of heat. So he stopped and asked if he needed a ride. The man enthusiastically thanked Jon for stopping and jumped in. He had arrived from Los Angeles several days before with three friends in a white Camaro. They had left him in Santa Fe and had promised to pick him up two days later for the ride to the Albuquerque airport. But he had missed them somehow. He asked Jon to drive around the plaza to see if the white Camaro was waiting for him. Jon drove around the plaza and along the streets within a two-mile radius of the plaza, but to no avail. It was obvious from the man's physical condition that he needed food and rest. Jon bought him lunch at a health food restaurant, gave him twenty dollars and took him to his house to rest. He left him there while he finished his own errands, and when he returned the man was in a deep sleep.

Jon was surprised to see that the man had ventured out to buy vegetables, and later he listened as the man told him how he had come up short to pay for the vegetables but that a man behind him at the checkout counter had offered him money to make up the few dollars difference. He went on and on with stories about how time after time he had been rescued financially by generous souls who, out of recognition of his divinity, had offered him just exactly what he had needed. Jon found the stories fascinating. He wondered if he had the ability to trust "the universe" if he were homeless and penniless. But it made him tired to think of it.

Throughout their dinner together, the man spoke of many interesting things, such as "spiritual super-synergy" and "cosmic metaprogramming." Jon listened, shocked at what he was being told, but unable to disbelieve. It was almost midnight when Jon began to see beyond the magic of the moment. The man told him that Jon had been chosen by God to take him to the Albuquerque airport and help him purchase a ticket so he could fly to India and save the "hundred souls still in captivity of the guru" he had left in Los Angeles. Jon excused himself to use the bathroom, where he thought about his choices. When he emerged from the bathroom, he told the man that he was not going to be taking him to the airport, that he could not pay for his trip to India, and that there were no flights leaving for India after midnight anyway. The man persisted, explaining how Jon had been chosen to do this great service.

Jon was exhausted, and after several attempts to say no, realized that he was not going to be heard by this man. So he excused himself, saying he had to get some rest in order to be prepared for work the next day. The man then accused him of being blinded by "temporal reality" and not attuned to the cosmic plan. Jon offered to allow the man to stay the night and went to bed. The next morning, the man's opened suitcase was sitting on the couch in the living room, but the man was nowhere to be found. Jon never saw him again.

Such a man is an example of someone who is flying but doesn't have a clue how to land, i.e., how to be on the Earth. I am sure it is true that many times he was rescued by a passer-by, or a customer at the grocery store, making it look like the universe was "watching out for him." Many of us rescue such beings when our path crosses theirs because they are painful mirrors of our own ungroundedness. If we "fix" them by throwing some money in their direction, we don't have to look at our own fear of homelessness or financial insecurities (ungroundedness). However, this man did not talk of the many times that he went for days without food or rest due to his inability to take care of himself. He did not talk about the times the "universe" did not take care of him.

Jon asked me if I thought he had been seduced by a vampire. I asked him to check in to see if he had felt exhausted or regenerated after his interactions with the man. He said, "I wouldn't say I felt regenerated. In fact, I was so tired by the time I crawled into bed that night, I could hardly think at all. But maybe that was because I was in the process of moving my office down the street."

I then explained to Jon that frequently people who have experienced a lot of kundalini energy or tantric mental, emotional or physical stimulation seem to be highly spiritually developed. But they are often spiritual addicts. They go from one spiritual "high" to another incessantly, but their feet barely touch the ground. They are barely here on the planet. When they are around grounded, integrated people, they energetically lean on or suck up their energy or ground support. This can take the form of asking, verbally or nonverbally, for food, money, or other things. This can be exhausting for the one being "sucked." It is another type of parasitic vampiring.

When we looked more closely at the moment Jon first saw the man on the street, Jon said, "Oh, I know. I'm still looking for that spiritual high. And I'm still looking outside of myself for spiritual joy. I was mesmerized by the sight of him. I thought, 'How interesting he looks. He must be a wandering sadhu (Hindu homeless holy man). He's doing something I've always been tempted to do.' But the next day I remember thinking, 'I've got a successful practice. I'm developing myself as a healer. I'm continually amazed at the miracles that happen in my practice.

This is everything I've ever wanted. Why do I want more?'"

Why did Jon want more? Ramana Maharshi, the famous Indian saint, said, "The only obstruction to enlightenment is the belief that there's an obstruction." We don't get much confirmation of our awakeness in Western culture. However, we get plenty of confirmation of our doubts about our awakeness.

The dysfunctional family is another example of a parasitic vampire. The dysfunctional family arranges itself around a designated dysfunctional authority figure. Everyone is handed a part in the family dance, and the pattern becomes fixed. When individuals only learn one move of the dance, they do not develop into whole people, capable of making choices about their own behavior. They simply act out of a conditioned reaction to life, depending on what aspect of the dance in their dysfunctional family they were given.

Claudia Black's model of the dysfunctional family is useful in understanding the parasitic pattern. She describes four basic roles that family members act out: the scapegoat, the hero, the lost child, and the clown. All four roles are ways of responding to what she terms "the elephant in the living room." The elephant is an authority figure who is dysfunctional in some way, maybe an alcoholic or a rageaholic (someone who rages compulsively). But no one talks about the dysfunction because they fear their fragile house of cards (their family) will fall apart. The child who is the hero usually achieves great academic, creative, or athletic feats in order to bring dignity and honor to the family to cover the shame of "the elephant in the living room." The lost child gets acceptance from the family by retreating into invisibility. The clown uses humor to make light of everything, again, to cover the shame and stay in denial of just how bad it really is. The scapegoat is the child who gets attention by acting outrageously. The scapegoat is usually the one who will risk punishment in order to do whatever he or she wants to do.

In my family of eight children, we had two sets of each of these roles. I danced the scapegoat movement of the dance. A friend once told me I was the pressure relief valve for all the righteousness in my family. I said what no one else would say. As an adult, I have had to apply deep consciousness to my responses to situations because my tendency has been to play the heavy in every group. Most of the time I haven't wanted to play the heavy, but it has been a conditioned response. I have continually found myself in conflictive situations just by saying what everyone else was withholding. As a child, the damage to myself was that I didn't get to be the hero or retreat into invisibility or get the laughs. These are all aspects of wholeness that we each should be able to express at appropriate times. But when each of us only gets to dance one part in the family, we become partial beings instead of whole beings. The part of me that wanted to express these other aspects was the part that got siphoned off (vampired) by the dysfunctional family system. I had to learn to live without parts of myself. This was fragmentation—certainly not wholeness.

Something happened to me at age nine that demonstrates the parasitic aspect of the vampiring that went on in my home. I recalled it for the first time as an adult in a therapy session when I was trying to deal with writer's block. I was trying to write about an incident that had occurred when I was nine, and I was very frustrated because my writing had become choppy and dull. It was so bad that it was keeping me from finishing a book proposal. Eventually, I gave up and booked a session with a therapist.

During the session in her office, the smell of ammonia stung my nostrils. I jumped up and looked frantically around to discover where it was coming from.

"What is that?! It smells like ammonia!" Then I started to cry and hyperventilate at the same time. "Lie back if you can." It was the voice of my therapist. "Look at me, Marty. Notice your surroundings. You're an adult, here, in this room, now. It's August 9, 1993. You're not nine years old. Stay with the body sensations. Smell the smells, notice your breathing. Let these sensations roll through you like waves. Keep your mind on the room. Look at me. Play both edges. This is the way to release the frozen adrenalin, the stored trauma and shock, without reidentifying with the story." She held one hand under my neck and the other under my sacrum, as if she were holding a baby.

The week before, I had been trying to write about the time my father had all eight of us lined up, facing each other in a zig-zag line from his bedroom to the bathroom. Buckets of what looked like blood were being handed out from behind the closed door. My oldest sister took the bucket, passed it on to my next oldest sister, who then passed it onto my brother, and so on all the way down to my youngest brother, who dumped the bucket into the toilet. He then filled the bucket up with water and passed it back up the line to the bedroom door. My father took it into the bedroom, and we waited until the next bucket of blood came out, repeating the process over again.

I don't remember how many times this occurred. We were told to be quiet and to stay there until we were dismissed. The only person not accounted for was my mother. I was certain my mother was dying. I wanted to see her! I tried to be as quiet as I could but could not keep from crying. My throat felt like it would explode. It hurt from trying to hold the tears back. I looked at my brothers and sisters. They were all scared and stone-faced. I remember how quiet we all were. The smell was so strong and the buckets were very heavy. The thin metal handle of the bucket left red marks and indentations on my fingers.

As I passed the buckets down, I realized I had smelled that smell before when we had to catch chickens in our back yard after Mom had chopped their heads off. Then we had hung them upside down on the clothesline to drain their blood. There had been six headless chickens with white bloodied feathers, hanging in a row. The green grass below had dried black with blood.

At one point, the buckets stopped. Very soon after, my father came out of the bedroom to go to the bathroom. I sneaked into my mother's room. She looked almost dead. Her face was totally white. I asked her what was wrong. She weakly mumbled something that I couldn't understand. At that moment, my father came back into the bedroom. He picked me up by the shoulders and threw me against the wall behind the stove that heated our house. He shouted, "Stay there until you're ready to repent!"

I decided that I would not repent no matter how hot it was behind that stove. The situation became a battle of wills at that point. I stayed behind the stove watching my brothers and sisters continue to pass buckets of blood down to the bathroom and back. The front of my arms and face burned like hell. But I wasn't going to move! I figured that if I died, it would make my father feel bad—and that was worth it.

Some time later my father emerged again from the bedroom, half carrying my mother. He told us very gruffly, "Get back, all of you!" And to my older sister, "You watch them. I'm taking your mother to the doctor." And he left with no more of an explanation than that. We were left to wonder if she was dying and what the blood was all about. I don't remember talking about it after they left. In fact, I don't remember anyone ever talking about the incident after that. I had a nightmare that night, and woke up screaming hysterically. My father came into the bedroom, turned on the light, and slapped me very hard across the face. There was no compassion or understanding. Only the slap across the face. I was in shock from all the events of the day. Afterward, as I lay there in the dark, I decided that I would never give my father the pleasure of seeing me cry ever again. And I didn't. No matter how hard he beat me or verbally abused me, I never again cried in front of him. Instead of breaking my will, he refortified it. But that was when I began stuffing my feelings and blocking the painful memories.

When I came home from school the next day, my mother was still sick, but strangely happy. No one said anything about the bucket incident ever again. Twenty years later, when my mother was dying of cancer, I asked her about that incident. She said it had been one of the four miscarriages she had had. At the time, I was relieved to know the truth. But as I had not yet come out of denial about the abuse I had sustained as a child, I didn't ask any further questions. Denial is a funny thing. It is truly an effective defense mechanism. Three years after my mother's death, I finally found the courage to face the blocked memories and feel the painful frozen feelings.

This incident exemplified several types of spiritual abuse. First, of course, there was the parasitic aspect of my dysfunctional family. Had I not broken out of line to see the truth that was not being told, I would have avoided the punishment behind the stove. The ultimate result was that I gave up my feelings. My family was the vampire. I gave up my feelings in order to continue to play the role of the scapegoat in the family dance. This was a very big price to pay to remain in the family dance. Without the balancing mechanism of feelings, my life compass got broken and I lost my connection to Self. I lost my way.

Second, this incident also exemplified spiritual abuse resulting from puritanism. My father would never have discussed my mother's miscarriage with his children because it implied sex. Of course, there were eight of us already. But I think he looked at us as a result of the act of procreation, which, in his mind, was different from sex. He saw procreation as simply God's will. However, I don't know why it didn't occur to him or my mother that asking us children to "ritually" help with the cleanup without understanding what was going on would leave us traumatized.

Third, the incident was also an example of ritual abuse. We were ritually lined up and forced to be silent while passing our mother's blood to each other. When I attended the ritual abuse survivor's group in Marin County, I heard a similar story from a woman who, as a child, had participated in rituals about which she had known nothing. Deanna recently spent a month at a treatment center where they used drugs and hypnosis to discover what may have been programmed into her psyche while she had been under the influence of the rituals she'd been exposed to as a child. The reason she admitted herself into the very expensive treatment center was that she was having strong impulses to kill anyone or anything—just to kill. Of course, she was mortified by these impulses, but she knew they probably had something to do with her horrible past. Through hypnosis and drug therapy, she discovered that, when she had been eight years old, she had internalized the instructions given to her mother by the priest at her mother's fortieth birthday ceremony. The priest had programmed her mother to kill some form of human life as a sacrifice for the next satanic ritual. At the time she admitted herself to the treatment center, Deanna was three months from turning forty. At eight years old, she had been standing nearby and had not been actively involved in the ritual. However, because of her strong identification with her mother, she had picked up the programming.

Children are so impressionable. They take everything in like a sponge. When they are traumatized, the trauma gets internalized even more intensely, like the searing of a cattle iron at the cellular level. Unfortunately, as a result, their natural defense mechanisms, such as the fight-or-flight reflexes, become distorted attempts to survive. The children become alienated or pseudoautistic with teachers and helpers. They are often labeled as having learning disabilities of some kind or another.

chapter four

Spiritual Predators: Let Us Prey

Who am I?
Sometimes when I speak,
I forget to move my mouth.

Sometimes when I see,
I don't open my eyes so that they can't see me seeing them.

Sometimes I hear so loudly,
People tell me it hurts their ears.

Sometimes when I smell the world real deep,
I taste those horrible brown shingles on that Montana house.

Sometimes when I touch you,
The only thing I can feel is fire in my veins.

When I run away from you,
I get lost inside myself.

Maybe I haven't grown into who I am yet?
Who am I?
—Poem to my first boyfriend: age 12

THE BEHAVIOR OF spiritual predators is more aggressive than that of parasitic vampires but can still be fairly subtle. Spiritual predators prey or stalk in search of opportunities to suck others' chi-juice. Any one of us can be drained when they prey on us. Unlike spiritual parasites, they know when they are being offered people's power and are willing receivers. They usually prey on people with weak egos who are likely to give their power away.

As the child of a spiritually predatorial minister, I was preyed on from day one of my life by being turned into an employee without pay. For example, at age two, I sang for the first time with my family. We sang the Negro Spiritual "Amen." It was perfect for a two-year-old since there was only one word "amen" to remember throughout the entire song. But someone in the church had given me a piece of chewing gum. After watching my older sister play the accordion for a few minutes, I took the chewing gum out of my mouth and pretended to play an accordion by pulling my chewing gum back and forth between my hands.

My older brother, who was standing directly behind me, took it upon himself to reach down and grab the chewing gum from between my hands. Being two, I perceived this as losing something that was mine. I began crying very loudly, and one of my sisters picked me up and carried me out of church. There was a lot of pressure to be a perfect performer. Age two was simply too young to be expected to sing professionally.

I never had much say about the jobs I did in the church. I was at the beck and call of not only my father and mother but also the church members. And what's worse is that when someone would compliment me on my singing voice, my father would say, "Don't believe them and get a big head, Martha. Your voice belongs to God. It doesn't belong to you." I was an employee of religious predators without pay. I was being used by the church. Another incident that occurred when I was an employee of our singing evangelistic family was one that I never forgot.

It was a hot Sunday in July of 1963. I had just turned thirteen. It was 98 degrees Fahrenheit in that one-hundred-year-old church in that small town in Indiana and it was only 10:00 a.m. The day was a scorcher! The air was heavy with humidity. The strong musty smell of the hymnals and the dark oak pews was stinging my nostrils, and I was starting to bleed. I had three older sisters whose menses I had witnessed, and it had not seemed like a large deal. I had just expected to take it in stride when it happened to me.

That Sunday I was leading the congregation in a song, "There is Power in the Blood." I noticed how white my knuckles were as I hung on to the pulpit to steady myself.

I could feel the blood running down my legs.

There is power, power, wonder working power, in the blood of the lamb...

No one had said that menses would cause nausea. I was determined to get through the song. I didn't know what I would do after that. How could I make a graceful exit with blood running down my legs? I was supposed to lead the congregation in three songs. This was only the first. My voice was getting weaker and weaker. So I sang louder. I could feel the veins in my throat engorged with blood as I forced the sound from my throat.

There is a fountain filled with blood drawn from Immanuel's veins.

The highly arched windows began spinning slowly. I clung to the pulpit.

Mine iniquities so vast have been blotted out at last. There is power, there is power in the blood.

Then I remembered the previous Sunday when I had refused communion for the first time. We had previously learned the passage in Deuteronomy in which the men were instructed to refrain from "touching a woman with 'issuance' (menses) because she was unclean." When I heard the communion stewards say, "Drink all of it; for this is my blood," I was repulsed to think of drinking Jesus' blood. My father noticed that I had refused communion, so he walked to where I was kneeling and asked why I had refused. I told him the same thing I had heard other parishioners say: "I have an impure heart." It was understood that if one partook of communion with an impure heart, the consequences would be worse than if you never took communion at all. People had reported a deluge of tragedies after taking communion when they hadn't been pure of heart. My father angrily motioned me to the altar to "get a pure heart." I followed him to the end of the pew and then bolted toward the door. My dog, Sheba, was waiting at the church door, as always, and we ran down to the railroad tracks and sat waiting to jump onto the train, which never came. I went home and was later deeply humiliated by my father, who preached at me in front of the other family members about how much I needed communion.

So, having received his rebuke the previous Sunday, I felt I had no option but to remain on the platform through the end of my duty, despite my bleeding. My voice barely audible, I tried very hard to remain standing. Then I felt myself leaving my body, floating up toward the highly arched ceiling. I looked down on that girl, who was me, clinging to the pulpit. The congregation started moving toward her. I saw one of them hungrily lapping up the blood that had fallen onto the floor. Another poked the engorged vein in her throat and put his mouth over it. I saw her body fall, and then I couldn't see her anymore because the people descended on her.

This was a hallucination from feeling faint. However, it was a perfect metaphor for what I was experiencing as a thirteen-year-old being ritually abused by Christian fundamentalists—spiritual predators—who misunderstood spiritual power to consist of dominance and control.

Another example of a spiritual predator from my youth was a minister with whom I once arranged a counseling appointment in the church we were attending at the time. I had wanted to talk with the regular minister, but he was too busy, so he called me to ask if the youth minister could stand in for him.

The youth minister was very good looking. The other women sometimes made jokes that "finally God had sent a good-looking one." He obviously loved the attention. I never felt safe around him, but I laughed with the others at the jokes. When I arrived, I asked if I could tape-record the session. He walked toward me and smiled, demurely tilting his face to the right. "We don't need to tape anything, do we, Marty?" he said. I explained to him that I simply wanted to be able to listen to the session later to get the full benefit of his responses to my questions. He, again very demurely, said as he walked toward me, "I guarantee you'll get the full benefit right here and now." I became afraid and told him that I just realized that I wasn't ready to talk about my problem. I left before he could respond. He was preying, or setting the stage for some kind of sexual energy exchange with me that he didn't want to go on record. I can't tell you why I was able to say no to him. My guardian angels must have been working extra hard that day. But I had been extremely uncomfortable in his office. I had felt the energy of his "preying" even though I hadn't known what it was that had felt wrong. I had registered it as unsafe and had flown out the door.

Because of my early conditioning to give myself away in service to the church, I was especially susceptible to spiritual predators. I lost my sense of self and later went looking for it in spiritual workshops, spiritual technique trainings, formal spiritual and theological education, and so on. After ten years of intensive searching, I tallied the amount of money I had spent. I concluded that it was somewhere between $135,600 and $150,000, depending on whether travel costs and lost wages were included.

Before I got wise to this pattern in my life, I got sucked in by many spiritual predators. One of my first awakenings occurred when I became part of a group that practiced a type of therapy called "deep process." For me, deep process was effective in the emotional release of frozen memories, such as those of my incest experiences. Incest seemed to be a common theme among the participants in that community.

At one point, I learned from one of the facilitators that the founder of the group made a sexual comment in one of the group sessions. She said, "She sure has a cute butt," when one of her clients was stomach down, sobbing on the pillows. Everyone laughed. This was a blatant misuse of power, and it was predatorial behavior in that the founder was using the group to express herself sexually. It was also spiritual incest and sexual abuse. It was spiritual incest in that the client was vulnerable at that moment, trusting the founder to keep things safe for her. It was sexual abuse in that her sexuality was being exploited on a group level, at a moment when she assumed it was safe. I talked with this client some years later about the incident. She said that she was so grateful that she had never become part of the founder's inner circle when such an opportunity had been made available to her. She knew that she had been so enamored of the founder's powerful wisdom that she would not have been able to say "no" to her sexually.

I later moved to the Bay Area to join a group of thirty-five people who were coming from all parts of the country to study with a popular New Age teacher. This teacher was offering an eight-month-long Creative Leadership Training. The experiences that I had had up to that time had surely contributed to my awakening to my spiritual addiction. However, the Creative Leadership Training was a real eye-opener. In fact, that experience caused me to finally come out of denial about my spiritual addiction. The vampiring that went on during those eight months was incredible. The blatant abuses that occurred would not allow me to continue in my denial: one woman was actually spat upon; there was emotional and physical violence in the group; and the facilitators were having sex with various participants. One of the facilitators asked to sleep with me. It was a brief tryst, but long enough to find out who was sleeping with whom.

Seeing these abuses firsthand gave me what is referred to as "the moment of awareness," the first phase in healing from spiritual addiction. It was the biggest pinch I had experienced. I could not close my eyes to the insanity of it all anymore, no matter how much I was getting from the creative opportunities. I realized that I had been governed by something outside of my awareness my entire life—namely, the spiritual fist in my back that had driven me to keep looking for something to fill the black hole. I looked back at my life and saw how this addiction had wreaked all sorts of havoc for me. I had run out of money. I had sold my car. I had no source of income. I had $128 in the bank to which the IRS had attached a lien. I realized that I could no longer continue in my frantic and costly search to fill the ever-growing black hole. I saw that I was going to have to "die to it." This meant that I needed to surrender to the fact that I was helpless, and to give in to the possibility and despair of never finding peace.

I could see the need for surrender, but amazingly, I was not quite ready for it. I had entered the second phase of healing, which is "bargaining." I bargained with myself. I told myself that the Creative Leadership Training had been a somewhat painful experience, but nonetheless an anomaly. I promised myself that I would be a better screener of truth the next time—that I would not be so gullible—that I would take the good and leave the rest.

Immediately following the Creative Leadership Training, I raised the funds so I could attend the nine-month Ancient Wisdoms School. The attendees were initiated into various esoteric traditions by shamans of each of those traditions. The traditions included Celtic studies, African shamanism, Navajo shamanism, Sufism, Gnosticism, Egyptian mysteries, Polynesian Kahuna, and Tibetan Buddhism. This experience was very interesting and good for me in many ways. I was able to see what Alan Watts referred to as the "perennial wisdom"—the wisdom that every major tradition has in common, such as unified consciousness, unconditional love, immortality, and forgiveness.

The founder was considered to be a great healer by many. She had a background both in science and philosophy. She was brilliant in some ways. The students were working adults who met each month for four or five days.

Each month the students were initiated into a different esoteric tradition according to the chakra that was being studied that month. *Chakra* is a word from the Eastern traditions. It actually means "rotating energy center." We studied the first chakra, which is located at the base of the torso and has to do with our physical existence or anything pertaining to the Earth, by being initiated into the Celtic tradition. We studied the second chakra, located in the abdomen and sacral area, where sexuality, sensuality and the emotional body emanate, by being initiated into African shamanism. We learned about the third chakra, which has to do with our sense of personal power and is located in the solar plexus, by being initiated into the Navajo tradition. We were taught about the fourth chakra, or heart chakra, which involves the higher emotions such as compassion, splendor, ecstasy and unconditional love, by being initiated into the Sufi tradition. The fifth chakra, in the throat area, having to do with creativity and full spiritual, physical, emotional, and mental expression, was experienced through our initiation into Gnosticism, the occult side of Christianity. (Note: the word "occult" actually means *without* cult.) The Gnosticism we studied included the Christian documents dating from before the industrialization of Christianity by Rome. We learned about the sixth chakra, located between the two eyebrows and having to do with our psychic powers, extrasensory perceptions, e.g., telepathy and visioning, by being initiated into the Egyptian mysteries. The seventh chakra, located at the crown of the head, and having to do with our connection to the nonphysical or spiritual realms, was experienced through the Tibetan Buddhist tradition.

This type of school was perfect for a spiritual materialist like myself. I could really get my money's worth of spiritual highs, which were like drug highs. The sad thing was that the founder of the school was a spiritual predator who was selling spiritual highs while preying on the students in search of her own highs. She had been clinically diagnosed as manic-depressive. But she hated losing the highs when she took her medication, so she stopped taking it and her condition went untreated. When she was high, no one could match her creativity, but when she was low, she made sure she took everybody down with her. She was both subtly and blatantly manipulative. When she was low, she used language to twist events around so that it looked very much like we, the students, were at fault. Through our bonds of fascination and affection for her, the group of all fifty-three of us were up if she was up and down if she was down. She played us emotionally, up and down the scale, at roller coaster speeds. We were the "charge" for her emotional batteries. My body often felt like an electric battery that had been completely discharged. It always took a long time to regain my vitality after being with this teacher. She preyed on and fed off of us. I am sure that the drama she created with us served to pump her adrenals in a sort of "self-treatment" way to regulate her brain chemistry. The group dynamic we all danced together was very covert.

In this group, the drama trauma of the day always seemed coincidental with the ordinary events of the day. But because I had been exposed to the manic-depressive pattern in other people, I began to see the up-and-down pattern and its supposed synchronous dramas. As soon as I became aware of this pattern, I saw that I didn't belong there anymore. The minute I got savvy to the one-way flow of energy from me to her, our dance stopped. I felt no more loss of energy. In fact, I became quite energized.

I asked myself how it had served me to be the supplier of this woman's energy. At first I had no answer. I could not imagine how it might have benefitted me to allow someone to suck my energy like that. Then I realized that the experience had given me the illusion of being mothered. This teacher had been a strong maternal archetype, and I had been very hungry to be mothered. Of course, the reality was that I had been sucked dry by a spiritual teacher.

Arthur Deikman writes brilliantly in his book, *The Wrong Way Home*, about the incessant need we have to be mothered and fathered. He explains that, because of this need, we get sucked into following shadowy spiritual teachers or cults. He illustrates his point with a "Peanuts" cartoon showing Charlie Brown resting in the back seat of the car on a Sunday afternoon's drive with his mom and dad. Charlie Brown says, "There's nothing as great as snuggling into the back seat while someone else drives the car."

Deikman discusses the phenomenon of cultism. One criterion of a cult is that its leader must be authoritarian in an almost military sense:

> *Authoritarians emphasize obedience, loyalty and the suppression of criticism of themselves. In*

> *the groups they lead, hierarchies or rank are emphasized and autonomy discouraged. (Sometimes such a leader takes a benign, "loving," tolerant position, but allows his or her lieutenants to enforce an authoritarian regime.)*

The reason that we adults allow such leaders to govern us is that our very primal need to belong was not met as children. In addition, the natural development of our autonomy may have been suppressed. We consciously or unconsciously continue to look for someone to parent us. As long as we unconsciously look for a parent, we cannot access our own inner authority. Arthur Deikman goes on to say:

> *We can trace our susceptibility to authoritarian leaders to the family structure, but in doing so we should not forget that the authoritarian character of the family is both functional and appropriate. Within the family, parents are in fact superior in knowledge, experience, and strength to the children who are dependent on them for protection and satisfaction of needs. As children mature, the hierarchical structure moderates and becomes more democratic in a healthy family.*

In deep grief one day after cutting my ties with the maternal teacher of the Ancient Wisdoms School, I realized it was time to grow up and recognize myself as the mother, the wise one, the one who knows. It was a painful lesson to learn. I am very grateful that I was given this lesson. It was the lesson that gave me back trust in myself, but it has taken a long time to heal from having been emotionally and spiritually bludgeoned by the founder of the school.

The Ancient Wisdoms School experience also helped me see that I was not going to find truth all wrapped up in one beautiful package and handed to me in one esoteric tradition. That was what I had been searching for all my life. The experience was interesting from an anthropological view, but it further confirmed my addiction to amassing multiple spiritual highs, which was costing me a lot of money. As I realized this, the black hole felt blacker and more bottomless.

I realized I had entered into a codependent relationship with the founder of the Ancient Wisdoms School. There had been an unverbalized contract that had said I would trust her to make my spiritual decisions for me if she would mother me. After coming to this realization, I went back to the Twelve Step programs and immersed myself in Al-Anon for awhile. I needed to clear that codependent pattern out of my repertoire.

The Twelve Step programs have truly been a cornerstone of my spiritual foundation. Out of them, so much of the healing of my soul has occurred. For the most part, these programs involve a beautiful community of people from all economic levels, races and creeds. I have found these people to be honest and humble, recognizing their need for help. They are not dazzled by the high ritual of religious pomp and circumstance. I have felt very safe with this community. But some of the concepts of the Twelve Step programs now seem spiritually limiting to me. For example, there is still an emphasis on a male God being "out there" in most of their literature.

The recovery community has its parasites and preacher vampires, too. There is one man in particular who is quite popular and often appears on television. Sometimes I turn the volume all the way down and just watch his body gestures. His arms flail about as he speaks. His face often gets very red. He slams his book down on the podium for emphasis. He is an angry man "puking his own process" on the Twelve Step recovery community. He is seductive because much of what he says has validity. He is brilliant and has contributed a great deal to the Twelve Step community. But the manner in which he shares information is parasitic in that he exercises his "power over" muscles and releases his rage on an audience that is so hungry for freedom from their painful codependency that they have all their receptors wide open. This is a misuse of power. It is spiritual abuse, and his behavior is that of a predatorial vampire. He telepathically preys on his audiences for power. The individuals in the audience look at him in awe. They give him their power by worshipping him and looking to him for their truth instead of inside themselves.

Sometimes dependency is fostered by sponsors. Sponsors are experienced Twelve Steppers who make themselves available to the less experienced for daily support, usually by telephone. It is quite common for Twelve Steppers to lose confidence in their ability to think for themselves. Because of that, the sometimes daily phone calls between sponsor and sponsees can become advice sessions. The sponsors are also recovering addicts of various types, so the validation that comes from being the answer givers is sometimes too great a seduction. The relationships between sponsors and sponsees then can become the sponsors' psychic food, that is, the good feelings about themselves. Stalking prey for psychic food is the behavior of a predatorial vampire.

I do not believe the Twelve Step community is fraught with too much vampirism. The Twelve Step traditions that are established in the literature do a fairly good job of keeping it in check. These programs are amazingly pure in spite of their patriarchal residue. My experience has been that there is a small percentage of people in the Twelve Step community who abuse their positions of power. After all, most people who join the Twelve Step community hardly want to be there. The reason they join Twelve Step programs is to heal the codependencies or addictions that have manifested in vampirism. Perhaps they simply could not protect their children from abusive fathers. Or maybe they caused accidents on the highway while they were under the influence of drugs or alcohol. These are also examples of vampirism in which real red blood is involved.

There is another way in which the traditional Twelve Steps foster dependency. The steps talk of a God who is male. In Western culture and many other cultures, women learn helplessness. This is "the Cinderella complex." We are taught that if men are real men, they will rescue women.

When girls appropriately mature into women, they go through what is usually a difficult period of throwing off this belief. The difficulty usually manifests itself financially. So if our spirituality (and the Twelve Step programs are spiritual programs) encourages women to "turn our will and our lives over to the care of God as we understand *him*" (third step), women have a natural expectation to be rescued. Of course, the rescue rarely comes, so women are often left with deepened anger toward God and men.

For men, the situation is sometimes just as difficult. All of their unresolved "father" issues can complicate the process. If a man had a good relationship with his father, he often benefits from a natural faith.

But a natural faith is not available to women when the gender of God is ingrained in the fabric of our society as male. Women's "natural" relationship with the divine, as it is handed down to us by parents and society, is fraught with many complications simply because the gender of God is male. Even if a woman had a wonderful relationship with her father, she may be unable to internalize God due to the fact that she is female and God is male. The answer is not to make God female but to understand that the divine source is both male and female. This divine source is within us, and is larger than male and female or any one of us as an individual. It is animate *and* inanimate, personal *and* impersonal. A mature spirituality, for both men and women, is one that accommodates all of these paradoxes.

chapter five

Spiritual Perpetrators

> *Like the bird,*
> *being stalked by the snake,*
> *cannot use its wings,*
> *so one cannot move or turn away.*
> —Dion Fortune

Spiritual perpetrators are the overt vampires, the ones who sometimes break the laws of the land in the name of spirituality. However, as obvious as their misuse of power is, we frequently rationalize it in the name of blind faith, trust, or some other pious dogma.

Prior to attending the Ancient Wisdoms School, I was living in Boulder. I had recently divorced my husband and had started a new job. My workaholism came to a head. I did not realize it then, but I was using my job to preoccupy myself to keep from feeling the pain of my divorce. In my workaholism, adrenalin was the drug that I used like speed to work beyond my normal capacities. The effect was that I was numbed to what was really going on. As a result, the grief from my divorce went largely ungrieved.

One day I found myself bent over in my office with a gut-splitting cramp. I called 911 and ordered an ambulance. It was then that I realized I had to change something fast or I was not going to be alive much longer. I could not tell whether the pain was in my heart or my intestines. It so completely covered my being that I could not identify for sure where it originated in my body. The problem turned out to be colitis, but by the time I figured it out, I had already decided to make some big changes. I had decided to move to California to join the eight-month Creative Leadership Training, referred to in the previous chapter. A month later, I moved from Boulder to Marin County, California.

The training program was very exciting at first. The participants were creative types but most of us were just opening up to our creativity. The majority of us were in our early thirties. The spirit of the group from the beginning was one of joy and play, for we had finally given ourselves permission to be as outrageous as possible in order to find our creativity. The leader was a successful author and highly acclaimed New Age teacher. Her book, which had a lot of truth in it, was what had drawn me to the group.

About one week into the program, I announced to the group that I would not be returning if we did not have an agreement that no one would come to the sessions stoned. I said that I wanted to experience my creativity in a grounded way rather than in some altered state. The leader responded by saying she thought that if anyone in the group needed to do some drugs, it was me. She explained to me that I had the biggest control issues of anyone in the group and that drugs would force me to let go of my control. She was successful at causing me to doubt myself just enough to fall prey to her negative judgement of me. So I actually considered what she was saying. I said, "But what about the law?" She said, "If we never go beyond the law, we'll never break new spiritual ground." There was just enough of a tinge of truth in what she was saying that I got hooked.

I was in agreement with her that the laws of our land must be continually questioned in terms of whether they have outgrown their usefulness. And I happen to believe that drugs are still illegal mostly because much more money can be made on them when they are underground, as was true with alcohol in Prohibition days. But questioning our laws is different from disregarding them altogether, which is what I experienced the leader as implying and the participants as practicing. There was much talk in the group about illegal activities and who got away with this or that. One man had a connection to the Mafia and offered to steal my leased car from me so I would not have to pay the buyout fee. These were people for whom spirituality was said to be their primary focus. However, in their minds, spirituality seemed to have nothing to do with the rest of the world.

There were other things that occurred in the Creative Leadership Training that caused me to question the validity of what was being taught. For instance, one woman spontaneously interrupted the group to spit on another woman who, in her opinion, was too afraid of everyone and everything. She called her "milktoast," "wimp" and "marshmallow." The woman on the receiving end of the saliva cried and shamefully sunk her face low into her knees so no one could see her crying. There were seven facilitators there that evening. Three of them were therapists, three others were breath workers and "hands on" healers, and the seventh was the leader. Not one person rose from the circle to stop the abuse. I was sitting next to the woman who was spat upon and felt the toxic energy coming our direction. I became nauseated and decided to get up and leave the building.

The leader's sexual molestation of one of our group participants, who happened to be a thirteen-year-old boy at the time she molested him, was the most processed topic. One of the therapists in the group was his father. I never once saw this man rise to his son's aid during the group discussions of the subject. This scenario was a replay of my mother not protecting me from my father.

The leader and the thirteen-year-old participant had been in Hawaii doing the drug XTC together. The leader claimed that it had been such a beautiful spiritual experience for both of them that it could not have been wrong. For her it had been the crone (age thirty eight) initiating the virgin boy. This was the spiritual context for her rationalization.

The boy never wanted to talk to her again. I witnessed him wailing in a process at a friend's house, throwing himself against a deck railing. He screamed in anger as he realized that he would never again be attracted to girls his own age. I heard many conversations about this outside the group. The participants were tired of processing the topic, and several of us realized that our own incest recovery had completely gone underground. The progress we had made prior to joining the group had been lost. We admitted to each other that we were going back into denial that the incest had ever occurred.

The leader's behavior was that of a spiritual perpetrator and soul murderer. My experience of her was that she was beyond reason and that her inner world was such a moral wasteland that she was compulsively compelled to violate the boundaries of young innocents in order to snatch their chi-juice.

There are many such groups around. I interviewed Rex, a member of a spiritual community that called their program The Work. The group follows a system of beliefs based on Gurdjieff's Fourth Way concepts. The leader of the group is an American in his mid-forties who moved to Colorado from the East Coast about fifteen years ago. In the East, he had been doing energy work on patients in a chiropractor's office. He is recognized by his students as having very special, deep healing powers. Most of his students are drawn to him for health reasons. This supposed "gifted healer" must have gotten ill himself at some point with alcoholism. He is rarely seen without a bottle of Jack Daniels close by. One of the philosophies he teaches is to love the one you are with as if you are married to that person. He sleeps with any of the women in the group whom he fancies. He tells the members that his "healing" energy is so intense that it has to be "run out" each night with sex and alcohol or he will get ill with it.

There are about fifty members of this group in a small Colorado town; there is also a ranch that houses twenty-five to thirty members in New Mexico. The members read no newspapers, watch no television and listen to no radio. They well understand that they are to do what they are told to do. The guru tells them which house to live in and how many miles to run every day for their spirituality.

Jogging is the cult's main spiritual practice. Many of the members do three sixty-mile runs a month in addition to their daily runs. There are frequent accidents, sprained and broken ankles, and knee, back, and foot injuries. Rex was seriously injured three times in one year. Once when a car hit him while he was jogging. But the injuries are considered a nuisance by the members, to be tolerated only until the moment their bodies are able to run again.

The group has wild parties each Sunday evening, sometimes starting as late as 1:30 a.m. Monday morning. Because the parties last until dawn, the teachers of the schools and day care centers often fall asleep while teaching. There is poor school attendance as a result.

At sixty-three years old, Rex had left a marriage and an affluent life as a real estate developer to join the group seven years before. Three years after joining, he moved to the center.

Most members are afraid to leave the cult for fear

they will not be able to make it on their own. They do not make their own decisions. Rex said that no one who left the group was able to be successful on the outside. "Arm pulls" and the I Ching are central to the dogma. Arm pulls are a kinesiology technique whereby a practitioner tests the strength of a person's arm after a specific question is asked. By "reading" the degree of strength in the arm, the practitioner determines the answer. When they use the I Ching, the ancient Chinese oracle, only certain people can throw the coins. The problem is that there is a fostering of dependency in that the students are expected to accept the interpretation of the ones doing the arm pulls or throwing the coins.

Rex had left the cult when I spoke with him. He was in a phase of withdrawal. He was angry about having been insulted by the leader in front of 150 people. He had disagreed with the leader about how the finances of the group should be managed. The leader had told him to shut up and that if finances were left to him, the group would be destitute and in the streets tomorrow.

When I talked with Rex, his anger had begun to cool, but he was still very angry. Having been a successful real estate developer prior to joining the group, he had given two houses to the organization and had promised a third. The night he went to the third house he had promised, to tell them they would all have to move out because he was going to sell the place, he tripped on the stairs and broke his ankle. When he told me this story, he said he realized that the accident was an outer expression of his unexpressed anger. He said if he had expressed his anger directly to the leader, perhaps he would not have had to hurt himself.

As I talked with Rex about his seven years with this group, I could tell that he was not allowing himself all of his feelings about the experience because he continued to rationalize why the group had value. He said he had learned about nutrition and cooking for the first time in his life. The leader had helped him find the courage to leave a twenty-two-year-old marriage. He had learned the discipline of marathon runs. It is always good to see the positive in any painful situation, but not if it keeps us in denial about the level of abuse. I was careful not to probe too deeply because I could sense that Rex was protecting his dignity and hiding his shame for ever having been snagged into the group in the first place.

I also found this denial of shame in Rajneesh disciples. Rajneesh was the Indian guru who owned ninety-plus Rolls Royces and was eventually forced out of America and other countries for his group's public sexual behaviors, tax evasion, financial fraud, and immigration charges. He claimed that his secretary had mishandled his affairs. But in the end, she called Rajneesh corrupt saying, "He sells 'blue skies called enlightenment' while craving more Rolls Royces."

My feeling is that Rajneesh was determined to upset rampant puritanism, first in India and then in the rest of the world. This was a worthy cause. Puritanism is defined in *The American Heritage Dictionary* as a "rigid adherence to a moral code and a hostility to social pleasures and indulgences." I believe it is one of the most destructive elements in any group or society. But one problem is that

Westerners and Europeans do not have the deep acculturation of inner-directedness that the East Indians have. There is deep respect for sexual energy in the Vedas, or holy Indian scriptures. It is seen as holy energy. This important base was missing in many of Rajneesh's followers. Because of this, his teachings backfired on him.

While I was in India, I spoke with many Rajneesh followers, all of whom told me stories of abuse. They said there were hundreds, maybe thousands, of followers who became HIV positive or contracted AIDS as a result of the rampant promiscuity in the community. These people were not allowed back into Rajneesh's ashram in Poona. There were also hundreds, maybe thousands of women who had to cope with abortions, sexually transmitted diseases, miscarriages, and unwanted pregnancies due to the sexual activities that went on in the group.

Only one of the followers admitted that it had been one of the biggest mistakes of his life to have hooked up with Rajneesh. Philip called Rajneesh the Enlightened Crook. He believed that Rajneesh was a realized being but that he had seriously misused his incredible wisdom hypnotically. Philip had been entranced by him for fifteen years. It was only after Rajneesh died that "the fog began to clear" as he put it. He spoke of his spiritual addiction, his compulsion to acquire spiritual "highs." He said that he has now realized that his level of spiritual maturity when he joined Rajneesh was the same as when he parted fifteen years later. He spoke of the deep grief he felt about all those lost years and his alienation from loved ones during that time.

Philip was also in great pain from having been ostracized by the Sanyasin (Hindi word for "renunciate") community as a result of his unpopular negative realizations about his time with Rajneesh. There was a large Sanyasin community associated with Poonjaji, a direct disciple of Ramana Maharshi and a realized being who lives in Lucknow, India, where Philip was living. Philip had been studying with Poonjaji for several months, and it was interesting to hear him articulate how different his experiences had been with Poonjaji. He said that Rajneesh had used obstacles rather than teaching the wisdom of silence to help people wake up. Perhaps this was why one renowned Indian guru who visited America referred to Rajneesh as a dark guru. She said he spoke to the personality rather than to the divine spark in his disciples.

Philip said he could still hear Rajneesh from the other side laughingly saying; "Just see if you can find the Self in the heat of your sexuality." Rajneesh had recommended to Philip that he follow all his desires to their eventual ends. He had said that this was the only way to be free of them. As a result, Phillip had met up with much pain and suffering. But when he asked Poonjaji about acting out his sexual desires in order to manage them instead of being governed by them, Poonjaji said, "When you want to put a fire out, do you pour more gasoline on it? Just be still and see how you naturally behave." Philip told me that every question he had ever asked Poonjaji had been answered with help to return to the one Self which could be found in his own inner authority, but that all his interactions with Rajneesh had left him feeling dependent on

Rajneesh's advice or wisdom.

Philip admitted that he had benefitted from Rajneesh's lessons, even though they had been quite devastating. There had been an issue of an abortion and some other sexually related trauma. I do not doubt that hard, but wonderful lessons were learned, but such "lessons" may have been used to excuse or condone the misuse of power. Another follower, after losing hundreds of thousands of dollars in the Oregon ranch experience, said, "Had I not been driven to the depths of my despair, I never would have woken up." She also said, "He, (Rajneesh), was creating people who were creative, and free and the American government did not like this. That's why they were determined to be rid of him." While there may have been some truth to this, she may also have been rationalizing his behavior. And her comment that Rajneesh "was creating people" made me suspicious that she may have been one of those people who had gone to sleep in the back seat of the car while it was being driven by Rajneesh. No one creates us. No one changes us except ourselves.

When Rajneesh was asked what really happened in Oregon by his followers, he simply said, "It's not as it appears." Such words are used by many great teachers who have an ability to see a bigger picture in situations. They see something entirely different from what appears to be happening on the every day level. There may have been just enough truth in his words that his followers continued to be lured in by him at great costs to their lives. I do not know if Rajneesh was a spiritual vampire. I never saw him or heard him speak. And many of his followers are beautiful people. But there were many beautiful people in all the cults I explored. Some people, however, felt that they lost many years of their lives and that they were deeply scarred as a result of their time with Rajneesh.

Whether the spiritual vampire is unconsciously parasitic, semi-consciously predatorial or the fully conscious perpetrator, they inevitably do spiritual damage. Fear and oppression are keys as to whether we are being vampired. Fear and oppression drain us of our vitality. If we feel drained after being with a person, then the chances are that we have been vampired. The physical body is a good barometer since it perceives things subconsciously before we realize them consciously. The questionnaires below will help you determine your level of seducibility by spiritual vampires and whether or not you have vampiring tendencies.

Are You a Victim of Spiritual Vampires?

1) Are you expected to think like your teacher, group, minister, or therapist?

2) Would it cause trouble if you told your teacher, group, minister, or therapist that you believed differently or disagreed with him or her?

3) Are you easily controlled by fear?

4) Are you easily controlled by guilt?

5) Does your teacher/leader promote the belief that he or she is the only one with the whole truth?

6) Does your group or teacher discourage questions?

7) Does your group or teacher claim that their way is the only way and that others who believe differently will suffer?

8) Does your group have rituals that it claims *are necessary* for salvation, enlightenment, self-actualization, or membership?

9) Does your group have an authoritarian leader? An authoritarian person is someone in a leadership role who presents him or herself as an *unchallengeable* authority.

10) Do you rationalize doing things you don't want to do with a spiritual group, therapist, or teacher?

11) Could your group or teacher be called fanatical by others?

12) Does your group try to control your money? your thinking? your behavior?

13) Have you given more money to your group or teacher than feels comfortable?

14) Have you quit your job or left your family because you "had" to follow this teaching or teacher full time?

15) Is your loyalty to your group or teacher interfering with your relationship with your children or spouse or other family members or friends?

16) Have you ever felt hopeless or that the only way "out" of your spiritual group or away from your spiritual teacher is suicide?

17) When your teacher, guru or spiritual group praises you, does your self-esteem go up?

18) Are you sexually attracted to or have you been sexual with your spiritual teacher, therapist, or minister? (*see note below)

19) Do you feel more comfortable with a list of "do's," "don'ts," and "shoulds"?

20) Do you sometimes feel tired or drained after being in the presence of your teacher, therapist, or minister?

*Feeling sexually attracted to your spiritual teacher is more of a red flag than it is a sign that you are a victim of spiritual vampires. In fact, it is common to feel sexually attracted to someone who is teaching you at the level of intimacy that spirituality is. But it is good to recognize that something entirely different could be occurring. One possibility is that the sexual attraction you feel is probably your attraction to yourself when you experience it mirrored in your spiritual teacher. If you lack a sense of personal empowerment, a second possibility is that you could be experiencing an attraction to the teacher's power and not to them personally. In any event, very few people in a position of leadership or power are spiritually savvy enough to resist the temptation to act on the sexual energy that surfaces in such relationships. When they do act on it, it is inevitably a misuse of power because the distribution of power is not equal. In such cases, the one with less power is always being taken advantage of.

Are You a Spiritual Vampire?

1) Do you have trouble being just friends with people? Do you have peer relationships in your life, or are you more comfortable being the spiritual counselor, therapist, or teacher?

2) Do you enjoy having power *over* others?

3) Do you enjoy it when others are humiliated or "put in their place" by a spiritual teacher?

4) Do you crave spiritual intimacy? Do you just have to have it no matter how new a relationship is?

5) Do you feel the need to be in control in spiritual groups or with friends?

6) Do you believe that spirituality is above the law?

7) Do you enjoy spiritually scaring or alarming people about their past, present, or future?

8) Do you feel uncomfortable when people come to their own truths without your help?

9) Are you sometimes totally bewildered by your behavior with others?

10) Are you inclined toward mental force or violence when others do not readily agree with you spiritually?

11) Is your life full of chaos and drama?

12) Do you spend a lot of time thinking about what you are going to say to others, practicing to say "the most profound thing"?

13) Do you "need" to be a spiritual teacher? Do you feel unfulfilled when you are not leading or mentoring?

14) Have you ever used your position of authority to force or persuade people to participate in rituals about which they have expressed fear?

15) Have you ever used your position of authority to force or persuade people to engage in sexual acts for spiritual purposes or for your own pleasure?

16) Do you demand that your children obey you only *because* you are their parent? Do you require that they attend spiritual events with you when it is obvious they are uncomfortable?

chapter six

The Seduction

> *We're like fish in the ocean desperately seeking a drink of water.*
>
> —Sri H.W. L. Poonjaji

Why are some people more susceptible to the seduction of spiritual vampires than others? One reason is being born into situations of compulsive religiosity that create spiritual addiction, as was true in my case. As a result of my upbringing, my level of seducibility by spiritual vampires was very high. However, we do not have to be born into compulsive religiosity or cults to have a high level of susceptibility to spiritual abuse.

A second reason for susceptibility is the desire to die.

This is not understood by those who have not suffered severe trauma. This desire is based in the lure of peace on the other side and the transcendence of suffering that death can bring.

A third reason is vulnerability. Sometimes life brings us to a point of such vulnerability that we are easily seduced by spiritual vampires who offer us love, acceptance, forgiveness, or some other quality that we crave at a particular phase of our lives.

A fourth reason is the unaddressed fear of death and the concomitant desire for immortality.

A fifth reason is the desire for power. This is such a complex trap that it deserves to be covered separately in the next chapter.

 Compulsive Religiosity

Those who have not experienced compulsive religiosity wonder how church can be as addictive as a drug. I have not had a lot of experience with drugs, but I have experimented to some degree. What I have discovered is that the "church high" can be as powerful or more so than the high obtained with any drug. In the fundamentalist Christian churches in which I was raised, methods similar to hypnosis were used as inherent parts of the church process. Much of what we accepted as "gospel truth" was merely suggestion that was implanted while we were entranced. My family used to say I was demonically possessed.

I think they believed this because I would not conform. I believe that, through the entrancement of the religious leaders, we were all possessed by the hypnotists who completely dominated our souls.

My first memory of being entranced was when I was five years old. It was a very hot day in July. We children had been sent to the chapel. The adults were in the tabernacle, which held about five thousand people. The chapel was packed with children aged five to ten. The songleader had us singing the Negro spiritual, "Them Dry Bones." We were standing up and turning around and bending up and down to demonstrate the song with motions. She repeatedly encouraged us to sing the song, over and over, louder and louder. It was hot; the chapel was packed. The songleader was using several classic hypnosis or induction techniques: repetition, muscle fatigue, and swaying motions (the muscles directly access the subconscious). We were turning around and around, bending up and down. I glanced up to my right where the sun was shining through the stained-glass window, creating a multicolored, pulsating shaft of light. I imagined that I could slide down the beautiful shaft of light. And there I was! I saw the children below, packed together, doing the motions to the song. As I was suspended in the air, the singing sounded far away. This was my first conscious recognition that I could leave my body. I thought God had "saved" me because I could fly. I thought that it was good to sing songs about God loudly while doing the motions because "that's how you could get saved and fly." I needed to be saved not only because I did not want to go to hell, but also because I was the minister's daughter. Annihilation in the psychological sense was always a real threat in my family.

It was after this experience that spiritual addiction became firmly rooted in my life. I began a long journey of attempting to reenact that experience of bliss. I would love to have the money I spent on retreats, workshops, spiritual therapists, classes, books, and travel with spiritual groups, trying to get back to that high. Thankfully, I finally stopped trying. However, getting to the point where I was ready to stop trying was a painful and dangerous journey. It triggered serious withdrawal symptoms, ultimately almost costing me my life. A "moment of recognition," which is one of the first phases of healing from spiritual abuse, came when I was twenty-four-years old. For years I had had no expectations of receiving anything spiritual from church. Church as a "drug" had lost its effect on me. However, I continued to attend. My use of the drug of regular church-going was only to keep me from going into withdrawal. I have heard drug addicts speak of their recovery from drugs this way. I was terrified to stop going to church.

This was not a rational fear. It was more like a primal fear. The ritual of going to church was so mixed up with my spirituality that the idea of not going to church seemed wrong—as if I would be without any spirituality at all. This was the lie of my spiritual addiction—that I would be bereft of spirituality if I gave up my addiction to church.

This is the case whether the spiritual addiction takes the form of worshipping a guru, meditation, going to church, or any other spiritual practice that we are attached to. In general, spiritual practices are fine. And church is also fine. However, I was using church and spiritual practices to find God *outside* myself. And I believed the practice was the thing for which I longed and searched so diligently. This distinguished my process as an addiction.

I had so many mixed feelings. The church had been my life up to that point. I loved the music (not the words) and the idea of being in a spiritual community, even though I never quite felt aligned with the people in the community. I hated the superficiality and the controlling energy. One particular Sunday, I scribbled a poem by Catalys, the Greek poet, on the back of a tithe card:

> *I hate and love.*
> *You ask how that can be.*
> *I know not how,*
> *But feel the agony.*

Agony! At that moment I became aware that the outer form of my spirituality—the church—was useless. I had been avoiding this moment of awareness, like a woman avoiding the awareness that she has stayed in a marriage seven years too long. I ran sobbing from the church and never went back again.

Not long after this, I realized that I was not happy at all to be without some sort of spiritual practice. I was solidly addicted to the outer forms of spirituality: meditation, ritual, the search for God outside myself. However, I was not aware that I was addicted. I just felt that life was not worth living without some sort of spiritual search.

Suicide was often not very far from my mind.

In an attempt to deal with my suicidal urges, which I later realized was a withdrawal symptom from my church addiction, I decided to study yoga. I thought it would bring me back to center. At the end of the first session, the teacher instructed us to bow to the person beside us in the circle and say, "I bow to the God in you." When the person beside me did this, I had a physical experience, as if a lightening bolt had gone through me. I later told my husband about it. He asked me not to return to the class, saying he believed it was "satanic." I didn't feel that way, but I trusted his judgment more than my own. So I quit going. I fell into suicidal despair once again. Years later I realized I had tried to use yoga in the same way a drug addict would have searched for a "fix" to relieve their pain. If the yoga teacher had been a spiritual vampire, I would have been easy prey for his seduction.

As at other times in my life, transformation was preceded by illness. Shortly after the yoga experience, I got very sick with acute strep throat and had to be hospitalized. Every day for eleven days, I was given a huge shot of penicillin in my hip. I was incredibly weak, and I moved in and out of delirium. One day, I had an out-of-body experience. While lying in bed, I experienced myself suspended three feet in the air, facing my body below. There were three white-robed figures in the upper left corner of the room. They extended their hands toward me, saying, "Come with us. We'll show you everything you want to know." I said to them, "I *so, so* want to go with you. More than anything, I want to go with you, and I just can't! I'm too afraid." I was very drawn to them but was also afraid that they were there to guide me through the death experience. My disappointment at not being courageous enough to go with them manifested in my body as excruciating physical pain in my heart. I cried a long time after I returned to my body. It was fifteen years before I could talk about this experience to anyone.

The Desire to Die and the Lure of Peace

Following my foundation-quaking, out-of-body experience, I fell into a deep depression once again and planned my death. I drove out to a tree in the country. I was going to drive very fast directly into the tree after dark. However, I was not able to follow through. I was afraid I would not die—that I would just be paralyzed or find myself in some other equally horrific condition. I clung for dear life to my therapist, increasing my appointments to three times weekly.

Formal analysis became my primary spiritual path for the next few years. I did not then refer to it as my spiritual path, but I read every self-help book and psychospiritual article I could get my hands on. I quit reading fiction altogether. My hope was that psychology, by virtue of its relationship to spirituality was going to give me happiness. Therapy did turn out to play an important role in my eventual surrender, which is my spiritual focus today. I had to go through the initiation of understanding the mechanics of my mind and its relationship to my body, spirit, and emotions before these aspects of myself could be surrendered as the blissful servants of consciousness itself.

With the help of my therapist, I made a commitment to live. He helped me look in all the corners of my spirit for thoughts of death. I realized my love affair with death on many levels. Even my language was fraught with this infatuation with death. I heard myself say things like, "I thought I'd die!" and "That house is so beautiful, it's to die for!" One day I was talking to an employee who wanted to present me with some marketing ideas. When she arrived for her appointment, I greeted her with: "I hope you're going to kill me with your ideas!" I gasped when I realized what I had said.

When I was a child, I was often given the duty of sitting with people in my church who were dying. Because of my reputation in the family as a tomboy, I never got the babysitting jobs like my five sisters. I felt as if it was almost a punishment to sit with the old dying people. I hated the smell. I can smell it to this day when I recall sitting with dying people as a child. It is a distinct smell that seems to accompany actual physical death. It is dark, moist, and musty, tinged with a slight smell of ammonia.

Eventually, however, I came to enjoy my time with the dying. I discovered that the only people I could trust to tell the truth were people who were dying. Most dying people were interested in completing unfinished business and were only interested in the truth. They were often very affectionate with me and grateful for my help. I also noticed that I felt forgiven when they died. I did not understand why. Now I understand that I was sticking my own toe over to the other side when they died. By virtue of my association with them, I was experiencing some of what they were experiencing in their passing. I was never afraid of this feeling. It was always peaceful and seemed very natural, like no big deal. They were mostly the elderly people of our church, but their deaths were interesting to me. I never told my family I enjoyed my task because I feared they would put me on some other less interesting duty.

Fascination with death must be dealt with. It often produces situations that can bring death. My fantasies of ending life in my car did manifest in a serious automobile accident. My best friend from childhood happened to be driving by when the accident occurred. She told me later that she had heard the medic say frantically, "We've got no pulse on this one. She's gone!" She heard a newspaper reporter ask for clarification, and the local newspaper reported my death the following day.

I did die—nearly. I felt like I was on a roller coaster. It was indescribably pleasant. The roller coaster was taking me upward in a spiral motion toward an enormous bright opening. The light was very bright but soft, like liquid spilling all around. Then there was nothing but this liquid light. There was no sense of myself, except as part of the liquid light. It was restful, exciting, pleasurable, and quiet all at the same time. There was a very strong sense of peace and love. I thought that my prayer for peace and rest had finally been answered.

But then I came to on the x-ray table. I asked the x-ray technician if anyone was aware that I was pregnant. She exclaimed, "Oh my God! We've taken full-body x-rays!" Then she ran out of the room. I was sure the fetus had been killed by the radiation. All at once the recognition of having been spilled back into my miserable life hit home. I was in unbelievable pain. I had a broken upper right arm, five broken ribs, a sprained back, a concussion, and stitches the entire length of the back of my head.

While I lay still, I recalled the car accident and that wonderful place I went while unconscious. My experience of being in that place was not unlike my experience of being upside down as an infant when I had whooping cough. It was not unlike the delirium of my bout with hepatitis. It was a deep, peaceful silence.

Ram Dass said that his disembodied spirit guide, Emmanuel, responded to his question about whether death was something to fear with, "It's like taking off a tight shoe." This was my experience, too. It was such a respite from my lifelong suffering. No wonder I did not want to go on living.

They put my arm in a hanging cast. I had to sleep sitting up until the bone in my right arm fused back together. The doctors told me that the fetus and the broken bone were vying for calcium, so it would take longer than usual to heal the broken bone. I was required to be still once again. The bone did not completely fuse until after my son was born five months later. The recovery period was very peaceful, however. It was as if I had a whole new beginning after touching in with the other side.

During that healing time, at first I was disappointed

that I had not died. Later, I developed the very strong feeling that "all is right with the world." Somehow I realized after my near-death experience that I could not be alive if God was not in me. This realization allowed me to see for the first time in my life that I was essentially good, rather than essentially bad as I had been taught. I developed a large degree of forgiveness for myself and others. This was the biggest gift of this near-death experience.

The deep silence and stillness of the recovery time after my "death" heralded the next phase of my recovery from spiritual abuse. I began gathering as much material about death as I could find. I wanted more understanding of death and of how to be free and happy as I had been during the near-death experience. But it was not enough. A year after the car accident, I still had not found a spiritual practice that was satisfactory. I came to the decision that there was nothing to quell the turbulent, dark waters of my soul that caused me to feel on the verge of physical and spiritual nausea most of the time. Once again, I began to plan my death.

My grandmother had committed suicide. This fact was part of my family's history, although it was one of the family secrets. My aunt broke the silence for me. Grandfather had been a minister, and had probably given Grandmother an ultimatum to "stop drinking or else." Grandmother was afraid of not being able to hide her alcoholism from the church people. Her alcoholism was also a family secret. She used to be very depressed, and would walk along the railroad tracks for hours in the evenings. She was contemplating her own eventual death. When she could no longer tolerate her addiction to alcohol, she hooked up the horse and carriage, drove it onto the railroad tracks, and waited for a train to come. She must have gotten drunk in order to have allowed the train to hit hard enough to kill her.

The church is supposed to be a place of refuge, healing, and forgiveness. The opposite is often true. Grandmother was a victim of spiritual abuse. And the same cycle of abuse of which she had been a part was now causing me to be in the precarious position of becoming a casualty.

My son was two years old at the time these thoughts of suicide were crescendoing to a loud blare in my mind. I needed to stay functional for him, but it was practically impossible. This emotional breakdown was directly related to having quit going to church. I was in major withdrawal from the spiritual highs that were so easy to come by in fundamentalist Christian churches. But I did not know it then. I felt like a lost soul suspended in the black space of the universe, with no roots or connections to anyone or anything.

This horrible feeling of rootlessness made me highly susceptible to spiritual vampires. At the time, I happened to hear about a spiritual teacher who was speaking on *The Tibetan Book Of The Dead*. He welcomed me with open arms to his spiritual community. He eventually offered to help me to die in such a way so that, in his words, "I would never have to come back." This idea was particularly attractive to me. I was in so much emotional and spiritual pain, I wanted to never have to face it again.

This was my first exposure to the Tibetan Buddhist's

beliefs about death, for which I have great respect to this day. However, his portrayal of the Tibetan teachings about death was very skewed, given his selfish exploitation of people like me who were suicidal. For example, he told me that I'd have to stay alive for awhile while we prepared my place on the other side. He asked for $1500 up front.

Death also became a spiritual vampire for me. As the mythical vampires have physically died and become eternal, they achieve immunity to death. This was my attraction to the beliefs this man was teaching. After death became a possibility, I saw life differently. I could feel myself simply let go inside of all my attachments. It was such a relief from the striving and struggling to which I was so accustomed.

I also became very fascinated with anyone who was proclaiming death to be our civil right. I agree that it is our right to end our life. But I don't believe there are many of us who are spiritually grounded enough to understand how to negotiate the terrain of death—the actual crossing over from this life to the beyond. And I believe that very few of us have the necessary degree of spiritual sensitivity to understand when it is truly our time to die.

The Native Americans seemed to know when it was time to die. They said their goodbyes to their families, headed off into the hills and sat without food or water until their soul left their bodies.

Fortunately, there was one attachment I was never quite able to let go of. The daily interaction with my young son was my link to life. As I cared for him, I looked into his eyes, knowing I was contemplating death. I heard him telepathically asking me to please stick around for him.

 # Life Crisis Vulnerability

Vulnerability is another reason that people are easily seduced by spiritual vampires. For example, Joleen was not born into a religious family. There was no pressure to be religious and not even any encouragement in her family to be spiritual. As a teenager, she had a lot of freedom to explore various churches with friends. Her neighbors were Pennsylvania Dutch. She participated in their love feasts (covered dish dinners) fairly regularly. Joleen's involvement with cults did not begin until she was in her mid-forties. At that time, she was battling child custody and property rights in a bitter divorce with her husband. She was at a crossroads. She had lost interest in her career as a medical technologist. The children were eight and ten and were becoming more and more independent of her. The pain of the divorce was bringing up all sorts of fears and painful, frozen memories of incest and molestation for the first time in her adult life. She had buried these memories successfully, but the pain of her divorce was opening the floodgates to all her unfelt fear and pain.

During this time, a friend invited Joleen to a session with a spiritual teacher. The teacher said that most people on the planet were committed to negative forces but that he and his followers were committed only to the light.

The teacher spoke of the ignorance of most people on the planet saying they were susceptible to aliens who stole their souls and entered them through their opened chakras to possess them. He said the possessed do not have eternal life when they die; they are lost forever. He promised to teach the group members how to keep their chakras clean and closed in order to protect themselves from the hoards of aliens wanting to use their bodies and souls for negative purposes.

Joleen's mouth hung open most of the time she was at the meeting. She listened to the teacher speak and was frightened that she was one of "most people on the planet without a soul who were committed to negativity and darkness." The ideas this teacher was presenting made her anxious and she thought of her husband and how brutally he had behaved with her. She was certain he was possessed by such beings. She paid the money that evening to become a student of the "light" teachings and a member of the group.

Joleen participated in the group for almost a year while her divorce dragged on and on. About six months after joining, she heard the leader discrediting one of the group facilitators by saying he had gotten possessed. This facilitator, who was very charismatic himself, challenged the leader and was successful in getting a quarter of the group to leave and follow him. The leader then sent a group of three men to break his nose and run him out of town! According to a belief of the group, the third eye and nose are the primary transmission points for the light. If the nose is broken, the light cannot flow in the body.

At this point, the facilitator's wife, who had decided to stay in the group even though her husband had been kicked out, discovered she was pregnant. The leader demanded that she abort the fetus immediately, saying it was hopelessly contaminated with the father's energy. When the woman refused to get an abortion, the leader had three or four members of the group try to force her into allowing them to perform the abortion. She was able to put them off for a few days and decided to find her husband and flee the state. They went to Colorado, but before they reached their destination, she began bleeding profusely and lost the fetus. She nearly died from the loss of blood before they could get medical help.

Joleen was very upset by this incident. She had become friends with the facilitator's wife and was very sad to see her in so much pain. But she was able to overlook the group's abusive behavior by telling herself that she was willing to give up friends if that was what it took to be filled with the light.

Joleen went for a private session with the leader to prepare for her own child custody hearings. Her husband and his attorney had used information on the cult to declare her an unfit mother of their two children. When she arrived at the office for the session, the teacher's assistant took the two children to a separate room. The man told Joleen that he could see an energetic collar around her neck. He said that her association with her husband, who was possessed by negative beings from another reality, had infected her. The collar around her neck was the means by which the aliens were controlling her every move, and the collar would have to be removed.

Joleen was quite frustrated to hear this since she had employed all the techniques she had learned in the previous months to keep her chakras cleaned and closed. But she was also aware how depressed she had been and that what the leader was saying seemed true. He laughed and said, "What we really need here is a penis. And I happen to have one!" He explained to her that the electric current of a penis stuck down her throat would blow out the energy of the collar. She looked shocked. He then said to her, "Do you want this collar removed or don't you? I really don't like doing this but it's the only thing that will clear your light body." He asked her to get onto the massage table and remove her clothes, since he could only see the blockages in her electrical currents if she had no clothes on.

As Joleen was telling me this story, she frequently laughed in a high pitched, almost hysterical manner. I asked her about the laughter because it seemed strange to me, given the horror of the story. She began to cry and admitted that the laughter was her way of looking past the shame of it all.

After he put his penis down her throat, the leader asked her if she had orgasmed. She said that she had not. He told her that she had orgasmed. She decided to agree with him, figuring that would end the session. She was very anxious to leave. He told her that the collar was removed and gave her instructions about how to keep it from being put back on by the aliens. He then told her that her two children had collars as well and that the same act would have to be performed on them. She paid him $175.00 for the session and left feeling quite concerned about the children's prognosis.

Joleen decided to wait before doing anything about

the children. Her idea was to watch them to see if there were signs of possession. She noticed that the children were very irritable and mean to one another. Her heart felt heavy as she thought of the solution the teacher was recommending—his penis! She decided to try to do her own "light work" on the children as she had been taught, but two days after the "removal of her collar," she felt her chakras open and vulnerable again and made another appointment for clearing, but this time with the teacher's assistant. After the session, another $175.00 was paid, and she left still wondering if she had been successful in clearing the children.

Two weeks later, the leader told Joleen that the collar was back around her neck and that they would have to do the process of clearing again. With much dread, she made another appointment. This time the teacher told her she was going to have to kneel in front of him. Once again, she said she had an orgasm even though she had not. After the penis "treatment," the man put his hands all over her body to test the electrical currents for blockage. He said, "Both you and your daughter have blockage everywhere in your bodies. We are going to have to put the penis in your vaginas."

The mention of his penis in her daughter's vagina jolted Joleen back to reality and caused her to deeply question what was going on. Had the leader not insisted on treating her daughter, she might have continued with the group. Joleen discussed her concerns with one of the members who vehemently discouraged her from going to the police with the story. Shortly thereafter, two of the members of the group issued threats to her by phone.

In the weeks following, Joleen met a man who became her boyfriend. He was very instrumental in supporting her through the leaving process. With his help, she quit attending the weekly meetings.

Two weeks passed. Then the leader left a message on her answering machine inviting her to attend a meeting to "iron out all the confusion and difficulties" as he put it. Her boyfriend strongly discouraged her from attending the meeting. He told her that the leader would probably discredit her in front of the entire group and get her to recommit to the program. He suggested that she keep a tape recorder near her phone and record all conversations with members of the group. He was right. When she did not show up at the meeting, the leader called her and threatened to have her kids taken away from her. He told her that the children were in desperate need of a clearing treatment and that he was "being led by the light" to come to her house and pick them up. She told him she had not appreciated his putting his penis in her mouth, that he was *not* going to do that to her children, and that she was going to the police.

The next day one of the members arrived and pushed his way into Joleen's house. He held her up against the wall and made her promise that she would not go to the police. He said that he was taking the children with him. He told her that the leader had written her off as hopeless and that she was never to show her face at the meetings again. Fortunately, the children were away at a friend's house. The man slapped her very hard across the face and spat on the floor before he left. When he had slapped her, her head snapped back and hit the adobe wall so hard she sustained a concussion. Even so, she ran after him, pounding on his back and screaming that he could be assured she would never be at the meetings again and that she had already given the tape of her phone conversation with the leader to the police. He turned around and began hitting her again. Finally, he left her in a heap outside her house on the sidewalk. It was at this point that her boyfriend gave her a gun and allowed her and the children to hide out at his house.

Joleen went to the police and was told that she could press charges against the man who had beaten her. But because she was involved in court hearings on child custody at the time, she decided not to. The police told her that by law she was considered "a consenting adult" when she allowed the leader to put his penis in her mouth and could thus take no legal action against him. However, they did visit the leader to question him about his sexual practices in the group. Joleen called the local reporter and the story was written up in the newspaper. Shortly after the publication of the article, the entire group of about fifteen members moved to Los Angeles. Joleen lived in terror for her life for some months following these events.

During our interview, Joleen recalled how powerful she first thought the leader had been, though she had simultaneously been uncomfortable in his presence. She had also been very attracted to his female assistant, who had been quite beautiful and intelligent, and had seemed deeply compassionate and sincere in her spiritual calling. Why had she been so susceptible to the seduction of the group? She had been in dire pain from brutal divorce proceedings and had been feeling very helpless. Through the mumbo jumbo of the dogma, the leader had given her false hopes not only of getting control of her life, but of becoming one of the few people on the planet with a soul and, therefore, of possibly becoming immortal.

There are two participants in any seduction: the person doing the seducing and the one being seduced. In addition to her neediness and vulnerability at that point in her life, Joleen's sexual addiction was flaring up in full force, which increased her chances of being seduced. Her sexual addiction took the form of seductiveness. And those who seduce are most easily seduced. Joleen had a very seductive way about her, which I experienced firsthand in our interview. She frequently tilted her head to the side, laughing coyly about things she said that were not funny at all, all the while glancing at me out of the side of her eyes. She also tended to dress quite seductively and had a long history of sexual drama that she shared with me in the interview. I could see how she attracted people to her and how the leader, in a way, had been a mirror of her own seductiveness. However, she seemed to be very unconscious about it. Her unconscious seductiveness and unmanaged sexual energy were very dangerous. They attracted a spiritual perpetrator and soul murderer.

Joleen still suffers from the effects of her experience. While attending a party at her house, I observed three members of another cult she had recently joined very aggressively proselytizing new members. Some people became so angry that they left the party early. I do not purport to know whether or not Joleen has found the enlightenment for which she longs. Only she knows. But it appears that she has joined another group with cult characteristics. They believe very strongly that they are the chosen few. They have a language (words and phrases with particular meanings) unique to their group. Such a language is the way a cult readily identifies who is one of them and who is not. They are organized around an authoritarian leader who also calls his belief system "light work."

A compulsive search for the light with strong denial of the darkness is what Ram Dass refers to as "toxic oneness." The New Age phenomenon is full of this "toxic oneness," which is characterized by an extremely exaggerated fixation on the light with an equal resistance to the dark. Spiritually, the dark and the light work beautifully together when we surrender to the truth of what is. However, there are very few examples of this resolution of dark and light in our world.

The Balinese culture is one of the few on the planet that has reconciled the dark and the light. I had an experience while visiting Bali that turned out to be an exquisite kind of spiritual medicine. It illustrated the appropriate balance of light and dark for me. I wished that Joleen could have been there to see and experience it.

Nyepi is the Balinese New Year. Celebrations take place over a three-day period in April. On the first two days, hundreds of people with elaborately prepared foods walk in procession to holy springs or to the sea to present offerings to the gods, goddesses, and demons for the New

Year. As they offer these gifts, they pray for the demons to come out. After two days of this, each community parades its bigger-than-life, papier-mache' demon through the streets and alleys of its village. The demon actually appears to be alive in its personification and lifelike movements, because the movements are made by community members underneath the platform upon which the demon sits. The demon's arms and legs float and typically, a handkerchief or hanging item of some kind waves in the wind. Music is played and songs are sung to instill in the demon all the mistakes made during the previous year. This creates a cleansing of the town. The people run their demon image through each intersection in their town to scare the "unseen" demons away. All of these giant demon images are amazing to see. They are often wrapped in bloody entrails and spew vomit and fowl-smelling liquids.

The people of Bali call the demons out. They are not afraid of them. In fact, they acknowledge that all is divine and that surrender to the divine in whatever form is the only "safety" there is. This ceremony continues until the midnight before Nyepi. It is not a mere ritual. It is part of a living religion that still serves the spirituality of the people rather than some centralized group of power-hungry religious leaders.

The next day, for twenty-four hours, there is nothing but silence, complete stillness, prayer, and meditation throughout the entire country. It is very difficult to imagine all of America silent for twenty-four hours! According to the Balinese, however, the New Year must begin with nothingness because all existence originates from nothingness. There are to be no lights, no fires, and no driving of cars. No work is done and no sexual or other sensual pleasures are to be indulged, including eating. There is no reading, smoking, or even leaving the house. Traffic lights are shut off. Sea ports are closed. All of this is done so that the malevolent spirits will think there is no life in Bali and will leave for good. Malevolent spirits cannot exist where no one can be found. What a mature understanding of silence and its impervious nature to evil!

The Balinese are *literally* silent on this day. In my own life, when I am empty enough for consciousness to flow through me unobstructedly, I consider this to be living in silence. It is not a lack of sound or activity, but of confusion and chaos. For me, silence is the void, God, Goddess, All That Is.

I participated fully in the Nyepi festivities. I called forth the demons like the best of them. I threw all my favorite demons, weaknesses and self-doubts into the giant, gruesome beings carried by the Balinese through the streets. I screamed and ran and sang along with the gamelan bands. Then I was silent. I fasted for twenty-four hours and was completely silent until dawn the following day. I met my friends for breakfast that morning and, upon seeing them, began sobbing uncontrollably. I had been suffering from severe diarrhea for three days and an incest memory had been triggered. I had had numerous incest memories before but had been free of them for several years. Always before, I had been left with intense pain for several days afterward. Now, during the Balinese festivities, I was not thrilled about the idea of having a "memory" in the middle of all the bliss. I also did not want the pain that typically accompanied a memory for days afterward.

My friend, Ali, a trained therapist, guided me through this experience with much care and attentiveness. He kept his eyes interlocked with mine and encouraged me to feel the feelings, see the images and know that my true nature was truth itself. I needed to understand that this energy was truth in a not-so-ordinary form, just like the demons called forth by the Balinese. Through the tears of fear, I experienced moments of intense physical pain in my rectum. Horrid images alternated with moments of blissful awareness that my true nature was consciousness itself. The process lasted about thirty minutes. Afterward I felt rejuvenated, ready to take a walk in the sun. I had never had such an experience.

Historically, my incest memories would come unannounced and last a week or two, sometimes a month. Then I would be functional for a few months before the next one would surface. The gift of Nyepi for me was the realization that demons (incest memories) are a different form of God-energy asking to be liberated by my refusal to identify with them as reality. What liberation! What freedom from victimhood! What freedom from the dualism of light and dark!

The only way a thought can be liberated, whether it be an emotional, mental, or physical thought, is to return it to its source. This is done by "being silence." In other words, not following the thought, but not repressing it either. The recognition that we are silence and that silence is the source of thought allows us to notice thought without having to be affected by it.

In assessing our level of seducibility, we need also to assess our ability to take care of needs within ourselves. Seduction can arise from many things. As in Joleen's case, it can arise in a moment of crisis from the hidden terror of our own dark side. Or it can develop from anything we need in the moment of seduction, whether that be security and safety, love and acceptance, compassion, forgiveness, or relief from guilt. Seduction does not occur when we take care of our own needs. For example, when we find compassion for ourselves from within ourselves, we are not so susceptible to the false compassion of others, done out of an ulterior motive of manipulation. Self-compassion is not self-pity. It is in the willingness to pray that compassion will find us and flow through us for ourselves. Self-compassion dispels the desperate need to find compassion from others. A desperate need for compassion increases our level of seducibility by those who would take advantage of our momentary weakness. When we know self-compassion, we also know the difference between true and false compassion in others. When someone is authentically compassionate toward us, we can receive it without pledging our lives to the giver as we are prone to do in the stressful moments of weakness in our lives.

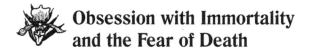

Obsession with Immortality and the Fear of Death

Even deeper than our unmet psychological or psychospiritual needs, our fear of death and subsequent obsession with immortality are very often at the root of our seduction by spiritual vampires. Many spiritual teachers advertise immortality as one of the main benefits of their particular belief system. The Christians tell us that if we behave in a particular way, we will go to heaven for eternity when we die. Many traditions offer immortality. And most of them teach that theirs is the only way to immortality. Immortality is a very strong pull for those of us who have not faced our fear of death.

The fear of death, which we must all face as part of being human, is a real impetus for many of the choices we make in our lives. However, it operates on a subconscious level for the most part. It is buried beneath all other fears, and it is at the root of all other fears. For example, our *unconscious* desire for an authority figure, a "mommy" or "daddy" to forgive us and make our spiritual decisions, arises from a time when we felt insulated from death. This need for a spiritual "mommy" or "daddy" is manifested in the world as a tendency to blindly follow a guru, teacher, or therapist who wants to do our spiritual thinking for us. As mentioned before, it creates the desire to sleep comfortably in the back seat of the car while someone else drives. The very *un*fortunate consequence is that we eventually lose our inclination to think for ourselves or have original thoughts, not original in the sense that they have never been thought by anyone before, but in the sense that the thinking is spontaneous and is done through us by consciousness itself. Without a fear of death our thoughts are fresh and of deep relevance to the moment. Our thinking consists of spontaneous thoughts rather than rote memories or deeply grooved patterns. Some people refer to these thoughts as revelations.

Facing our own death may be the most freeing thing we can do for ourselves. I had the good fortune to do just this while visiting India several years ago. Once there, I could not wait to get to the burning ghats (gates) in Banaras where bodies were being cremated. So I rented a boat and boatman to take me up the Ganges river. At one point, I saw the fires in the distance and asked if we could go closer.

At the cremation site, the families wrap their dead in a variety of sacred cloths and take them down to the Ganges river. Each relative then pours five drinks from the Ganges into the opened mouth of the corpse. The funeral pyre is lit by a five thousand-year-old fire that burns in a temple up the steps from the main burning ghat.

When the boatman hesitated to get closer, I said, "Please, I really must see it." So, he took me over to the boat that held all the wood for the pyres. The boatman gasped as I moved almost automatically off the boat onto the piles of wood, and then toward the steps, where I joined a family saying blessings for an old Brahman woman. "Swahi, swahi," (blessings) they chanted as they threw incense on the burning body. Without even thinking, I joined in the chorus of "swahi" as if I had done it many times before. The amazing thing is that I was not asked to leave. It was almost as if they expected me. I watched as the old woman burned. There was fire coming out of her ears. After three-and-a-half hours, they fished out the pelvic bone and threw it whole into the Ganges. For men, they throw the chest into the river. In the Hindu tradition, they regard these parts of the male and female bodies as the seats of the soul.

I could not stay away from the burning ghats. I returned three days in a row and witnessed five cremations. While I was resting on the train to Lucknow several days later, I fell into an altered state and experienced my own body going up in flames. It was as if I were watching my own cremation. I became clear that I was completely fulfilled without my body. I realized that I had a body but was not my body.

When we die before we drop the physical body, while we are still alive, we discover our true nature which is beyond our physical identity. We discover our divine nature, our whole selves. This is very freeing and empowering. Then and only then can life be lived fully. We discover that we are so much more than our small karmic existence or physical identity. Also, as so many people who have had near death experiences have recognized, death informs us of the preciousness of life.

Rene, the daughter of a Mormon bishop who had repeatedly sexually abused her as a child, was in the first phase of healing when I spoke with her. She had left the Mormon faith and was in shock, almost to the point of paralyzation, from her fear of death. In the Mormon temple, it is customary to make a gesture of crossing yourself before reciting the sacred covenants each Sunday. This gesture is not the Catholic sign of the cross. It is one big swipe across the throat, the breast, and the lower center of the body to signify that if you divulge any of the sacred secrets of the temple, you will be killed by God. Rene had broken her vow to God and the church to never tell the sacred secrets when she told her therapist all the stories of ritual abuse in the church. Unlike other ritual abuse survivors, who run from their perpetrators to safety, there was nowhere for Rene to run. God was omniscient—everywhere at once. And the fear of being killed by God had been imprinted in her cellular memory from the first impressionable years of her life.

When I first talked with Rene about the spiritual abuse, she told me her story in a broken voice, frequently stopping to cry and blow her nose. She was terrified to once again tell the secrets. From leaving the Mormon church, she was experiencing a deluge of withdrawal symptoms, such as feelings of isolation and despair. However, her biggest and most threatening symptom was her fear of death. She could not sleep. Her obsession with being killed left her with no tolerance whatsoever for her three children. She was afraid to drive anywhere for fear she would be in a car accident. She did have some minor accidents in her car during this time and eventually became immobile to the point of agoraphobia. Many times during that time of withdrawal, there were visits and letters from the people of the church attempting to persuade her to return to the church. She seriously considered going back just so she could get some sleep. The temptation was so great that she had to steel herself against it. The spiritual vampire, her church, knew how to use her fear of death to keep her coming back. Fortunately, she had a therapist who helped her resist the temptation.

In 1994, I was working with a client in my prosperity

consulting business who was highly susceptible to spiritual vampires due to her fear of death. This was ironic, because when she called me, she was very suicidal. Over a period of ten years, she had spent tens of thousands of dollars she had scraped together to pay for counselors, therapists, doctors, and psychics. She was deep in debt, which is what brought her to me. Her fear of death was manifesting as an irrational fear of contracting AIDS. It was irrational because she rarely had sex with anyone. But her fear of death caused her to suffer from many unidentifiable illnesses that neither Western medicine nor alternative medicine could address. She told me that she knew they could not help her long before she quit seeing them. But when she talked to one of her doctors about this, he became defensive and told her that it was her lack of trust in him that prohibited him from helping her. So the healthcare and spiritual-practitioner vampires kept milking her financially even though it was obvious they were not helping her. She had survived satanic-cult ritual abuse in childhood. Her terror of death was so powerful that she needed help to keep it from wreaking havoc in her life.

I was willing to help her as part of my own practice of tithing 10% of my time to gratis service. But I was wary of helping her because even though I was not charging her, I did not want to perpetuate a dependency on me. I could feel her desperately clinging to me as I was sure she had clung to the other healthcare and spiritual practitioners. But I was fascinated, as I am with all of my clients, and wanted to explore the root cause of her mysterious physical ailments that were draining her bank accounts. The first thing I noticed in her language was her obsession with death.

I intuitively decided to take a different tack with her. It seemed as though she had spent enough time and energy resisting death. And she was physically depleted. What would happen if she surrendered to death and found a graceful way to die? After many conversations about death, we eventually came to a point where she saw death differently. She saw it for what it was: an option, a real choice that she could make. This took some of the terrifying mysticism out of it and left her with a feeling of empowerment. Then we imagined together what it might be like for her to die. She used left-hand writing to dialogue with death: she asked questions by writing them with her dominant, right hand and responded to the questions with her non-dominant, left hand. She suddenly recognized that the energy of her left hand with which she was dialoguing was what some would call God. In her words, "God was just dressed up like death." When she came to this realization, both her fear of death and her desire to die began to disappear. It was a pleasure to work with her and hear her long sighs of deep relief as she reconciled with her own death. The last time I talked with her, she admitted that the mysterious illnesses still surface at times. But now when this happens, she dialogues with the illnesses and can usually hear what is being spoken to her through her body. The illnesses come and go and are much less frequent.

I was fortunate to witness what hospice people refer to as a "lovely death" when I was about thirty years old. When my mother learned she was dying of lymphoma, I volunteered to be the one to sit with her. I did not quite understand why I was willing to take time out from a career in marketing with the airlines to do this. But it turned out to be one of the richest experiences of my life. My sisters and brothers all thought it strange that I should be the one, given that I was the least amicable with our parents. However, it turned out to be a transformative event for me. Once again, I allowed my family to be grateful to me for attending the death process, not saying a word about my enjoyment of the process for fear they might want to be there themselves.

I had been out of contact with my family for some years and decided this might be an opportunity to mend fences. That was how I justified it in my mind. And I did get to complete unfinished business with my mother. However, now I believe that my decision was based more on my fascination with and fear of death.

My mother shared things with me on her death-bed that she never shared with anyone else. The Christian dogma fell away. She became as real as I have ever experienced her. She told me of the recurring rape nightmares she was having. After listening to these dreams, I came to believe that my mother had been a victim of spiritual and sexual abuse.

We did some visioning and drawing together. She drew herself walking toward a cliff carrying a placard with "death" written on it. She laughed as she narrated the story: "I can either throw the placard over the cliff or jump off myself." A few days went by before we returned to this process. She could not decide what the last frame of this drawing would be. Finally, she confided in me that she simply could not draw the last frame. She said, "I want to die but I can't put it on paper." She had consciously surrendered to her death.

Shortly thereafter, my father told me that she was gone, as far as he was concerned. He said that she mumbled incoherently out of her mind most of the time and that the sooner she died, the better for everyone. But that was not my experience. I sat beside her bed in silence for hours, not wanting to read or distract myself in any way from what was happening. It was very peaceful to be with her. Yes, she often mumbled words that apparently had nothing to do with her waking reality, but later when she would tell me her dreams or what she was thinking, her mumbled words made total sense. I could see very clearly that she was taking care of unfinished business in her spirit and mind. I was quite interested in this process and kept a journal handy so I could dialogue with her when she came to.

My father told me not to speak of her emaciated condition to the other siblings. They had all recently come from various parts of the country to visit her, and he had decided that we would just keep her worsened condition to ourselves so that they would not feel they had to spend money to see her once more before she died.

She was staying at the first hospice center in the United States at Methodist Hospital in Indianapolis. There was a doctor there on special assignment from Johannesburg who was training the staff. He and I had a couple of wonderful talks about death and the dying process. He asked me one day why I thought my mother was hanging on. He said that she had not responded to any stimuli for a week or voided (expelled water or waste) for three days. There was no physical reason she should even be alive. When I told him that she had mentioned about ten days earlier that she was not dying until she saw each of her children one more time, he strongly encouraged me to tell my brothers and sisters. I told him what my father had said. This was the only time I experienced the hospice doctor as a little angry. He said, "We have to keep our focus clear, Marty. Your mother is asking us to help her have a dignified death. We can't treat her like a child. It is our job to communicate her wishes to her children for her process of completion. What her children do with that information is between them and her. It's not our business."

With this encouragement and support, I phoned each of my brothers and sisters. Within forty-eight hours, they were all at her bedside. My sister who had recently given birth was the last to arrive. She arrived at 10:08 p.m. She carefully put her newborn infant near my mother's face as if to introduce them to each other. At 10:20 p.m, my mother took her last breath. I sighed a deep sigh of relief. With the help of the hospice staff at Methodist Hospital, we had successfully given her as dignified a death as possible. She had taken her last breath as she had wished, with all of the people she had brought into the world surrounding her.

That night I drove to the country to stay with in-laws. As I was driving, I was overcome with grief and pulled the car off the road to allow the sounds and sobs to take over. I got out of the car and lay across the hood on my back. As the sobs began to quiet, I opened my eyes and saw a shooting star. Then another and another. I counted twenty-one shooting stars in just those few minutes. Later, I realized it was August 8, around the time of the Perseid meteor showers. But I did not know this at the time. I felt very deeply that it was my mother saying thanks for tending her passing with such care. This experience brought me to a recognition of my passion to be with dying people.

I later joined the staff at the Living and Dying Project in Northern California to further explore access to the other side. I wanted to prepare for my own death by supporting people to live fully during the dying process. I wanted to die while still alive so I could fully access all levels of my being.

In my experiences with dying people, I have come to understand what the phrase, "lovely death" means. A lovely death occurs when dying people recognize who they really are. They realize that they are so much bigger than their physical bodies that are falling away. They see that death is just another moment of life. Therefore, they relax into the many gifts that death brings them. This is when immortality is really possible. Immortality is the state of being in which there is no death—no beginning and no end of life. It is the awakened state.

To achieve this awakened state, the death that must occur need not be a physical death. Waking up to the truth of who we really are creates the state of immortality. Once we recognize who we are, we realize there was no beginning and there is no end to our essentialness. The clients I was assigned at the Living and Dying Project were beautiful beings who shared this learning with me.

Try this exercise. Take any fear that may be currently plaguing you and dive into the center of it. In other words, be willing to feel it as deeply as possible. Follow the worst-case scenario in your imagination, asking yourself, "What if the worst possible thing happened?" Then push the situation further in your mind, asking, "And then what if this happened?" Keep pushing it further. What you will inevitably find is that beneath your apparent fear is another fear of something else. And beneath that fear is another fear of something else. Finally you will discover that underneath all your fears is the fear of death. Be willing to experience your own death. This is what the great Indian sage, Ramana Maharshi, did at age sixteen. One day he realized how afraid of death he was. He lay down in his room, imagined his death, and discovered that he existed beyond death. This was the moment of his awakening.

This chapter has described four ways that people are vulnerable to the seduction of spiritual vampires. Each of the four has the same root: the ultimate seduction of God's representations in human form. These representations can be gurus and spiritual teachers. It is much easier to believe in something bigger than ourselves that is immortal when there are awakened human beings in our presence. We know and long to confirm the presence of a bigger picture or plan than our small physical or karmic existence. As long as awakened beings (gurus and spiritual teachers) are physically alive, we more easily rest in the knowledge that yes, there is a God. But often, when their physical forms pass, as all forms do, we lose touch with our knowing of something larger than ourselves. We then frequently lose our connection to spirit, fall into despair, and look for another guru who claims to be channelling God.

A fifth way we are often seduced by spiritual vampires is through our desire for power. This is a very big trap, and is covered in the next chapter.

chapter seven

Desire for Power

> " *There are similarities between absolute power and absolute faith: a demand for absolute obedience, a readiness to attempt the impossible, a bias for simple solutions—to cut the knot rather than unravel it, the viewing of compromise as surrender. Both absolute power and absolute faith are instruments of dehumanization. Hence, absolute faith corrupts as absolutely as absolute power.* "
> —Eric Hoffer,
> *The New York Times Magazine*, April 25, 1971

SPIRITUAL VAMPIRES LOVE PEOPLE who crave power. We are easy prey because of our craving. Those of us who have felt powerless most of our lives tend to get fixated on accumulating power. We make especially good fruit for the picking because power comes in so many forms. There is the kind of power that comes from what Buddhism calls "spiritual materialism." This power leads to knowing how to fly without knowing how to land. There is the kind of power that creative visualization offers through the use of the mind. There is the kind of power that comes from one of the most contradictory sources: playing the victim or martyr role. There is the kind of power that Reverend Moon offers through his group. And there is the power that comes from serving others. The compulsion to serve from a selfish motive of power is what Ram Dass refers to as "toxic service." Some of these activities in and of themselves are not necessarily bad. But because they confer powers, we mistakenly assume that the powers are what fulfill us spiritually. We get derailed from healthy spiritual paths by our search for more powers. This infatuation with powers makes us highly seducible by spiritual vampires.

Spiritual vampires are often very charismatic, eloquent, and personally powerful. I interviewed dozens of people at various stages of recovery from emotional, financial, and sexual abuse by spiritual teachers and therapists. Common among their stories was the recognition of some attraction to the teacher's and the therapist's power. This attraction to power in others is usually a result of not being able to fully see ourselves and claim our own power. Most of us did not have parents who were strong or mature enough to acknowledge and mirror back to us our mental, physical, and spiritual gifts. As a result, we often cannot see our own skills and talents. Therefore, many of us are like sailboats without sails. And we are usually very willing to give all our power to the ones we want to emulate the most.

Learning How to Fly Without Learning How to Land

When I was nine years old, I had a wonderful introduction to extrasensory powers. I used to sneak out of my house to visit Haddie Cravens, the town witch. She lived one long mile away, especially long on a hot summer day. I used to wear rubber thongs that were particularly great for popping the beaded tar bubbles on the road as I walked to Haddie's. It was a sort of walking meditation as I anticipated her display of extrasensory powers and wise counsel. She used to greet me with a chuckle and, "Oh, it's the Christian man's daughter." I would sit with her as long as I dared, and she would tell me the most incredible stories of what she had done with her powers. I was in awe of her, and had my own experiences to corroborate her stories. Once she spit on some warts on my fingers, said some strange words, and the warts actually fell off! I was so taken with her, I once gathered ten other children from the neighborhood to visit her and watch her move tables and chairs with her mind. As a child, I longed for this kind of power and sought to understand it. These desires continued into adulthood and contributed to my vulnerability to spiritual materialism and my seducibility to spiritual vampires.

We all have spiritual powers, which we come by naturally as we mature in our spiritual growth. These natural by products of spiritual maturity include intuitive powers, the ability to see auras, telepathy, blissful states, and so on.

Sometimes people who are amazingly psychic or intuitive become spiritual snobs in their newfound powers. They have great contempt for those who live day-to-day, mundane existences. Underneath this contempt is usually their hurt from having been unsuccessful in the world. This lack of success, in turn, is due to weak ego-strength from childhood abuse or trauma of some kind. People with healthy egos usually know that they can be spiritual *and* happy in the world; they do not have to seek self-aggrandizement through spiritual powers.

A compulsive search for power often manifests in learning how to fly without learning how to land. This is common among those of us who suffer from weak egos. After recognizing that we possess some spiritual powers, we leave the world behind, not realizing that these powers do not give us the freedom for which we long. This condition is a result of the lack of integration of spirituality into the physical world, and is a formula for crash landings. I have known many seemingly wise, spiritual beings who cannot pay their rent, feed themselves properly, or keep jobs. They get evicted from their homes or get into serious debt before they realize they must take care of themselves on the physical plane. If their crash landings are painful enough, they wake up and recognize their addictions to the spiritual trappings of power.

This is what Trungpa Rinpoche, the late, famous Buddhist teacher from Boulder, Colorado, referred to as "spiritual materialism." Trungpa treated this subject comprehensively in his book *Cutting Through Spiritual Materialism*. We deceive ourselves into believing that we are on a path to develop our spirituality when instead, as Trungpa says, we are strengthening our egocentricity through spiritual techniques. When we practice spiritual techniques out of a notion of wanting to achieve a particular state of consciousness, we separate ourselves from the reality of who we really are. Ram Dass calls this "toxic oneness." It is an imbalanced focus on the state of unity consciousness or "the one" without an appropriate inclusion of the many states. An experience of authentic unity consciousness is one that includes our whole being, not just our more highly evolved states.

Any state, whether it is bliss or misery, is just that, a state. It comes and it goes. It does not touch who we are. All states rise out of consciousness. We are consciousness. States rise and pass through us. If we cling to a particular state, we stop the flow of energy. I once heard Gangaji, an awakened American woman and disciple of Ramana Maharshi, define addiction as the preference of one state over another. When we wake up, we learn the value of accepting and surrendering to all states, rather than clinging to or identifying with any one.

However, Trungpa says we sometimes try to collect spiritual experiences like antiques:

> *We may feel these spiritual collections are very precious. After all, we've studied so much. We have achieved and we have learned. We have accumulated hoards of knowledge. We display*

our knowledge to the world and in so doing, erroneously reassure ourselves that we exist, safe and secure, as "spiritual" people.

Spiritual understanding is not something we can collect. Rather, it is a remembering of the truth inside us. This remembering can be facilitated by an embodied teacher, or it can come as a revelation from our own knowing deep inside us. If it is stimulated by an embodied teacher, we often call it a "transmission." This term can be misleading if we take it to mean that the truth is outside ourselves. However, we can be inspired by awakened beings to remember our own truth. It is often this inspiration that causes us to awaken. One of the reasons I trust Gangaji is that she says again and again, "See for yourself. Don't take my word for anything. You must have your own experience. This knowing does not come through your intellectual understanding. Try it and see." She consistently sends me back to my Self.

The phenomenon of knowing how to fly without knowing how to land can be illustrated with the chakra system in the human body, as taught by the Eastern traditions. There are many chakras, but the basic seven, along with practices to develop their associated powers, are described on the adjacent page.

The heart, the fourth chakra, is the place of alchemy where spirit meets matter when the lower three chakras are integrated with the upper three. If people develop the lower three chakras to the exclusion of the upper three, they follow their instincts without the tempering of con-

CHAKRIC POWERS

Chakra	Bodily Location	Practices	Powers
1st	Base of Spine	Walking Meditations & Deep Relaxation Techniques	Comfortable on the physical plane. Bodily knowings, shivers, deep relaxation. Hair standing on end.
2nd	Sacram	Peace & Well-being Meditations	Contentment. Comfortable with sexuality and emotionality. Orgasmic.
3rd	Solar Plexis	One-pointedness of Mind Meditations	Comfortable with ego and personal power. Strong self-esteem.
4th	Heart	Rose Light of Love Flower Meditation	Deep love. Rapture. Bliss. Forgiveness.
5th	Throat	Toning & Listening Techniques	Heightened audio capabilities. Charismatic speaking. Persuasive powers. Prolific creativity. Bliss.
6th	Forehead	Christ Consciousness Meditations	Sees clear pictures, symbolic or literal. Past life memories. Telepathy. Sees auras and precognitive information. Bliss.
7th	Crown	Unity Consciousness Meditations	Receptive to whole concepts which include all the senses. Out of body experiences. An experience of one's immortality. Bliss.

science or spiritual values. If people develop the upper three chakras to the exclusion of the lower three, they often develop great gifts of charismatic speech, telepathy, or aura reading, but have no interest in doing what it takes to pay the rent. They sometimes become the powerful spiritual vampires, for they seek power in order to attract followers who will serve and care for them on the physical plane. Flying in the upper three chakras can be so tantalizing that it causes some people to have little interest in taking proper care of themselves. If there are enough spiritual "wannabes" around to take care of them physically, they never have to crash land. But if we, the spiritual power wannabes, emulate these teachers, and we are not charismatic enough to attract spiritual "wannabes" around us, then we eventually have a crash landing. Life catches up with us. Of course, bottoming out in our compulsive search for power can be an incredible gift. It can teach us that an imbalance exists that must be corrected, but the pain of correcting this imbalance can be devastating.

I recognize that some people are called to be of physical service to *awakened* beings. By "called," I mean that everything in their lives has led them up to that point. They can do nothing else. This is different from spiritual power wannabes who hang around the guru indefinitely to get a "hit of bliss." Wannabes look for darshan or the grace of awakened beings like drug addicts looking for a fix. If people are called to serve the physical needs of an awakened being, then that is their karma, or life-growth path, with all the typical challenges for growth built in.

Elaine, a friend of mine, told me a story of going for

the fix in a relationship with a man gifted with many *siddhis* (powers). She had met Ron when she was teaching a workshop and was very anemic at the time. She experienced him sending her energy so she could get through the day. Later, she discovered his other tremendous psychic powers and gifts. Shortly after the workshop, he called to ask her to dinner. On their first date, she noticed the incredible healing power coming from his hand when he put it on the small of her back as they were being seated at a restaurant. She experienced it as an electric surge. When they were having dinner, he stopped talking midsentence and looked at her. She was sipping her coffee, and she heard him telepathically say that the coffee was partly why she was exhausted all the time. She questioned him, and he confirmed that this was the message he was sending. Telepathy turned out to be one of their favorite ways to play together. He was quite intuitive and adept at scanning her and other people to obtain information he could never have gotten otherwise.

After they had been in relationship for four months, Elaine noticed that she was becoming annoyed with how needy Ron was. He needed her help with what she considered basic things like decision-making and self-approval. When she worked with him on making particular decisions, she often felt tired afterwards. She vowed to herself to stop enabling him in these areas. After all, she did not want to be his mother (his grounding). On the other hand, she was delighted at how light she felt with him, not so preoccupied with day-to-day stuff. He was one of the first men in her life who supported her psychic talents and intuitive knowing. She was so impressed with his special abilities that she considered dropping her writing ventures to support him in getting his spectacular gifts out to the world. She said it seemed as if God was saying to her that this was the way to go.

Earlier in their relationship and before they had made love, Elaine asked Ron if he had any sexually transmitted diseases and he had said no. Then one day he asked her to look at his penis because he thought he might have a herpes outbreak. She was confused and asked him why he thought he had herpes. He said the spot on his penis just looked like herpes to him. Elaine did not see anything to worry about. Later that day, they made love without protection. A week later she discovered she had genital herpes. For weeks, Ron acted as if he didn't have a clue how this could be. But eventually, Ron confessed that he had known that he had had herpes for ten years.

After much grieving about contracting herpes, Elaine realized that her experience with Ron was like that of a woman who had found a giant diamond on the road, strung it on a necklace, and hung it around her neck. Many people admired the exquisite, giant diamond. But then, behind her back, they commented on how bad she looked, bent down from the weight of it around her neck. Eventually she took the diamond off, but was never quite able to stand up perfectly straight again. Her body (grounding) took the brunt of the dangerous liaison with Ron in the form of herpes, a permanent physical malady.

Ironically, Ron is a doctor. He has powerful healing gifts, but he gave Elaine herpes. He is confused about what he wants to do with his life, so he does not practice medicine. He inherited a substantial amount of money when his father died. So money will insulate him from his lack of grounding for awhile. He is good looking and intelligent, so he will continue to find women to be sexual with him and provide his grounding for him. But Elaine will have herpes for the remainder of her lifetime.

Ron is similar to incredibly powerful spiritual teachers whose upper three chakras are highly evolved but who rely on their groupees or cult members to take care of them on the physical level. Some people may look at these great spiritual teachers and say, "But these people are very successful and do not have to be in the world." I say, show me people who are apparently successful and highly evolved in their upper three chakras without the proper foundation of the lower three and I will show you people who are vampiring the energy of those around them for their own grounding on the physical plane.

I once heard Diane Fassel, author of a book on workaholism, say, "You can't have transformation without recovery and you can't have recovery without transformation." This is another way to express the phenomenon of "learning how to fly without learning how to land" or vice versa. Transformation without freedom (recovery) from the slavery to any and all of our addictions, including the addiction to power, is flying without knowing how to land.

Recovery (sobriety) without transformation is also impossible because the root cause of any compulsive behavior (addiction) is deeper than the substance being abused. Many of us discover in our recovery process that when one addiction is cleared, another pops up. The term "dry drunk" refers to alcoholics who no longer drink but display all the old manipulative and controlling behaviors that allowed them to drink excessively in the first place. The "dry drunk" or person who recovers from substance abuse but not from addictive or compulsive behavior, is the person who learns how to deal with the physical plane (landing) but does not see the value of developing higher consciousness (flying). This is recovery without transformation.

Most of us are drawn to Twelve Step programs out of a need to stop our addictions. In his book, *Stage II Recovery: Life Beyond Addictions*, Earnie Larson claims that there are two stages to recovery. The first stage is retrieving our sobriety. Sobriety in this context is the absence of intoxication, whether it is with food, drugs, alcohol, gambling, relationships, or a myriad of other things. Sobriety brings with it an ability to be in touch with and accept our world as it is whether we like it or not. It does not mean that we do not still want to change some things. It simply means that we are in touch with and choose to surrender to life on its own terms. This is recovery without transformation.

However, at some point, if we are lucky, we realize that sobriety is not enough. We long for the healing of our separateness from God and other human beings. This is the longing to wake up to who we really are, the transformative feeling of "going home." The Twelve Step programs are the most effective way to retrieve our sobriety with respect to drugs, alcohol or food, even according to Western medicine. However, real and lasting happiness, joyousness, and freedom come from waking up. The tenth, eleventh, and twelfth steps are the steps of transformation. When we take these steps, we come to a resolution with power. Our experience of power is then no longer one of *having* power but one of *being authentically empowered*. Power flows freely through us. We no longer seek power, or anyone or anything to have power over.

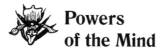 **Powers of the Mind**

One way to discern whether your teacher is a spiritual vampire is to see if he or she is seducing you with a promise of extrasensory powers or supernatural experiences. Spiritual vampires love people who want these powers because they easily become dependent. This was the temptation for me when I joined the eight-month Creative Leadership Training.

The New Age spiritual teacher and founder of the training program emphasized what we came to call "the resurrection of our greatly atrophied third eyes." This resurrection was the process of using our creative visualization powers to create our own reality. She spoke of the need to take big risks, to be outrageous and nonconforming, but she never spoke about how to integrate our newfound creativity with the rest of our lives. As a result, among the thirty-five participants, only a few were financially stable after the eight-month program. We had fallen into an illusion of security and abandoned any concern for our future during the eight months. After the eight months, we frantically searched for a means of income. This illusion of security was the dependency that served the needs of the spiritual vampire or teacher. As was mentioned earlier, she used the group to process her own crisis with the thirteen year-old participant with whom she had had sex.

My eight-month experience in that group was painfully instrumental in coming out of denial about my spiritual materialism. I do not know what I was thinking at the time. I knew that money was finite—that when you spent it, it was gone until you replaced it with more. But I had recently divorced my husband of fourteen years, who had been more like a brother and father than a lover. When I divorced him, my view of the world changed 180 degrees. I had been extremely dependent on him emotionally. I would make very good money, but I would not even open the envelope my check came in because I was afraid to discover that it was not enough money. I joined the creative leadership training out of a desperate need to develop my own source of masculine energy to function successfully in the world. I thought the technique of creative visualization was going to give me this power that I felt I lacked. But I was erroneously searching in the spiritual trappings of mental powers.

When I first heard the founder of the program speak about the connection between expressing our creativity and being able to manifest our dreams, I justified the tuition of $8,000 by concluding that I had been responsible in other areas of my life to the exclusion of expressing my creativity. However, doing the opposite, being true to my creativity to the exclusion of all my other responsibilities, caused me to be dangerously ungrounded in the world.

This turned out not to be the answer either. What I ultimately discovered at the conclusion of the eight-month program was that my lifelong compulsion to collect spiritual experiences was a compulsion to gain personal power.

My dreams of creativity always had to do with writing, speaking, dancing, and healing. Unfortunately, the Creative Leadership Training did nothing to further these dreams even though its emphasis was on creativity. In fact, the ending of the program brought about a great depression in me. I realized later that the group had provided me with the illusion of mom, dad, and siblings all having a good time, being outrageous with very little concern for what was going on in the rest of the world. In fact, we considered the rest of the world a mess, and looked on it with contempt. Of course, none of us in the group had any interest in actively changing the world. We mostly wanted to avoid it. This lack of integration with reality was an example of "learning how to fly without learning how to land." It was very dangerous. It was a regression to a carefree age when we had no responsibility. This isolation or lack of connection to the collective consciousness had negative consequences with respect to our abilities to take care of ourselves in the physical world.

The Creative Leadership Training was effective to a degree. Many of us successfully created things we had longed for in our lives, situations that through the exercise of creative visualization, we were able to bring into the manifest world. However, everything else seemed to go out of kilter to make space for these arbitrary creations. For example, one woman consistently visualized the knight in shining armor who would rescue her from her financial problems and marry her. Her knight showed up shortly after the eight-month program. However, he turned out to be physically abusive to her. This was the out-picturing of what Prince Charming looked like in her subconscious. Even though he eventually asked her to marry him, as she had visualized, she was not at all happy in the relationship. In the meantime, she had passed up an opportunity to take a lucrative position with a large corporation in her profession in order to live near this man.

There is nothing wrong with visualization or exploring our psychic abilities. For example, visualization is an important first step in manifesting what we need or want. However, I prefer to use the exercise of visioning rather than visualization. Visioning is deeper than visualization. Whereas visualization is the mental process of visualizing something we need, visioning accesses an inner state of reflection and includes mental, emotional, and spiritual pictures, symbols, and ideas. For example, if the woman who visualized her mate had been facilitated to reflect on her dream in the context of her whole life, she might have discovered that she was not internally ready for a life mate. In Lynn Andrew's book, *Medicine Woman*, her Native American teacher, Agnes Whistling Elk, gave her the assignment of going to the wilderness alone and remaining there until she was able to see inside her self-lodge to observe how the male and female were relating. What Lynn eventually saw was a male and female fighting with each other. She saw how this war inside herself had created so much of the negative drama throughout her life. She recognized that it was time to resolve the war between masculine and feminine energies inside herself, especially if she wanted to attract a loving mate who could travel with her in true love and support.

A good metaphor for visioning is of the monkey trap—a coconut shell with a hole in one side and rice in the bottom. A monkey inevitably puts his hand in to grab the rice but discovers very quickly that his hand cannot be pulled out because his clinched fist is too large for the hole. If he figures out that all he has to do is turn his fist over and open his hand, his hand *and* the rice will come out of the hole very easily. This is an appropriate way to participate in the co-creation of our lives through visioning. The receptive open hand, rather than the closed, grabbing fist, is the necessary posture of surrender to the highest good of all beings involved. However, without this understanding of the need for mental, emotional, and spiritual surrender, our creations become arbitrary things in our lives. In other words, they are not rooted in the foundation of our *whole* beings. As a result, the things we create are usually only temporary and do not meet our needs in a holistic way. An example is the woman visualizing a mate who turned out to be a mate she did not want at all.

Exploring our psychic abilities in an ungrounded or partial way can be dangerous. I had contact with several of the Creative Leadership Training participants two years after we completed the program. Not one of them had yet stabilized in terms of secure housing, income, or right livelihood. We had all been blown out of the water by the emphasis of the group on creating our own realities. We had lost our moorings.

Yes, transitional life changes sometimes do this to us, and it is sometimes necessary to lose our moorings. "Losing our moorings" happens when we cling tenaciously to the status quo and are unwilling to let go of the old. However using our psychic abilities out of the context of the rest of our lives is a dangerous misuse of power. And besides, transition does not have to be hard. When we are grounded, it can be an enjoyable experience without drama and suffering. Without these distractions, transition can bring many gifts and deep transformation.

Halfway through the eight-month program, I told the group that I needed to leave because I was running low on savings and was going to have to begin working full time. The response I got from the group was amazing. The leader told me I was running out of funds because I was not participating fully in the group. She told me that if I spoke up more and became more a part of the group, the universe would naturally provide me with the necessary funds to stay in the group. Looking back, I can see that her abandonment issues were at stake. She did not want anyone to leave.

One of the participants offered to give me $3000 so that I would not leave. Some of the other participants had discussed the same issue of low funds and had been given money by one or more people in the group. So I took the gift of $3000 and continued on in the group, rationalizing that I really needed to practice receiving help from others and to finish this venture rather than "be a quitter." I resolved to speak up more often and become more active in the group. But when I spoke up, I experienced the group as more interested in preserving its hierarchy of power than in looking at the truth. The group had classic cult-group dynamics: the hierarchy of power was contingent on who had the strongest personality. The quiet people rarely got heard, and when they did speak up, it was clear that they really had no say in the way things were going to be done in the group.

A few of us met with the teacher to discuss money issues toward the end of the eight months since she had claimed that creative visualization was the answer to a lack of money. The meeting was not that helpful. She advised me to borrow money. I was devastated. As mentioned earlier, I had $128 to my name, no car, no job, and no income.

I realize now that I created all that trauma for myself by searching for siddhis (powers) rather than my Self. I was looking for all the wrong things in all the wrong places. I looked for personal power and I looked for it in people outside myself who appeared to be spiritually powerful.

If that was not enough trouble, I later learned that the woman who had given me the $3000 was sexually attracted to me and that the $3000 had been her attempt to buy my affections. When she discovered that there was no hope of a sexual relationship with me, she claimed that the money had not been a gift but a loan. Of course, there had been no verbal agreement or documentation to this effect as would have been the case had she and I been grounded in the real world. This was an inappropriate use of power on her part. I would never have accepted the money on a loan basis. I was indignant at this point and felt totally manipulated. But because I was not in the least interested in any close relationship with her, she began harassing me on the phone, in my home, and on the street. I had to find an attorney to clear up the mess rather than try to communicate with her because her intense emotional and sexual needs were prohibiting any possibility of resolution. My attorney was finally able to get her to settle. But this is an example of the kind of drama trauma that gets created from focusing on flying to the exclusion of landing.

Another example of my infatuation with the powers of the mind was my exploration of EST (Erhardt Seminar Training). After just a couple of meetings, I got very excited (high?) thinking that controlling my thoughts would allow me to be happy and end my suffering. Of course, thoughts do not lend themselves very nicely to control. Mental pressure simply builds up.

There is a profound difference between mastery of thoughts and control of thoughts. Control of thoughts involves power *over* them so that inevitably they are repressed. Mastery of thoughts involves power *within* the self rather than power *over* thoughts. With mastery, nothing is repressed or indulged. There is no rejection of thoughts and no following thoughts. Mastery only comes as a result of recognizing who we really are. As we wake up and realize that we are not our physical identities (karmic incarnations) and that what we are is awareness (consciousness itself), our minds become the blissful servants of consciousness, blissful because they can finally relax! Before this happens, we think we are our minds, and we expect our minds to keep everything under control. This is an illusion. Our minds are merely computers. They cannot think original thoughts. They are very useful, however, when they are activated by consciousness, which is much bigger than our physical identities or our individual, karmic, incarnated selves.

At the time I studied EST, I thought it could free me, and I was willing to give it my best efforts. I worked hard with the friend who had introduced me to EST to word things differently and to push myself beyond my comfort zone. However one of the facilitators was very domineering with me. He said, "God, you're lazy! You have got to get control of your ego! You need to stand up in front of the group next week and ask them to help you kill your ego." While I believed what he said at the time about the ego, I could not hear it from him. My power needs bumped into his power needs. I was not going to expose myself to the criticism of three hundred people. I had witnessed others go through this treatment, and all I could see was that they came away with was bruised egos. He was a young EST zealot with a superiority complex who was exercising his "power over" muscles and puffing himself up or vampiring energy by disempowering desperate seekers through criticism and coercive language. Because of this, I lost interest in EST.

This negative experience with EST was further corroborated when I interviewed a man in 1993 who had lost $267,000 to the EST management group. I met him at a book store in a small northern Californian town. As we spoke, his eyes darted around the room in hypervigilence. I asked him what he was afraid of. He said that he was gathering information on one of the founders of EST, for his suit against him, and he was afraid that the town was filled with EST followers who might leak the information. He was so uncomfortable that I became uncomfortable and offered to meet with him elsewhere, but he felt that EST followers would be everywhere in Northern California. So we continued our interview under stressful conditions.

This man spoke so softly that I could barely hear him. He dropped his papers frequently, and moved quickly to pick them up and rearrange them even though the corners and edges were so badly bent and frayed that they did not lend themselves to order. My heart broke as I observed this man's energy. His shoulders were humped, and he looked at me from the top of his eyes because his head was bent down. He could not sustain eye contact. He complained about having been beaten psychologically in the EST practices. He claimed to be permanently psychologically disabled. I believed him by the looks of him.

I later went to this man's house to pick up some newspaper articles he had promised me. His living quarters were very damp, dark, cramped, and disorderly, with mountains of papers piled everywhere. If this man ever had any self-esteem, it was now almost completely gone. He said that he had given money on a regular basis over the five-year-period that he had participated in EST. He had been promised a career in management, but if that is true, it had to be a manipulative ploy for his money. I know that I would never have offered him a leadership position in any business I have ever been involved with. He was very intelligent and obviously had excellent research skills, but he suffered from little or no ego-strength and was desperate to feel personally powerful to the tune of his entire family inheritance of $267,000.

At this point in my life, I understand that the ego has its place, like the body or anything else on the relative plane. Killing the ego does nothing but perpetuate suffering. The ego is part of the vehicle of this personality on the physical plane. It is a necessary part of development. I like to think of it the same way I would an arm or a leg. That way I am not inclined to expect it to do more than it is designed to do. I believe the ego is designed to contain the persona—the image we portray to others—and the personality. Without an ego, a person isolates from others. And like the mind, the ego can also become the blissful servant of consciousness. This is the proper use of the ego.

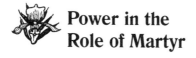 ## Power in the Role of Martyr

For most of my life, I was desperate for freedom. And since I had been so oppressed, I thought freedom was power. My obsession to gain personal power drove me to try every spiritual experience that crossed my path. In my quest for power, I became a Christian fundamentalist, a Jesus freak, a Wiccan and Native American initiate, a member of EST, an avid Lifespring and metaphysics student, an initiate of nine various esoteric traditions in the Ancient Wisdoms School, and a participant in ten years of Twelve Step programs. Yet, I never found lasting spiritual fulfillment. I would have bouts of suicidal thoughts throughout my search when I would inevitably discover that "that" wasn't it either. Therapy was a constant for me until the early nineties and was instrumental in keeping me alive during my long spiritual quest.

At one point, I gave up on my spiritual search and decided to solve my restlessness by turning to a career. This was not an easy path either. The negative moralism associated with working mothers in my family was very strong. My family believed that if mothers went to work they were abandoning their children. I realized later how much of a lie this was because, as a minister's wife, my mother *was* a full-time working mother. I remember many times when she simply did not have time for us because she was preoccupied with the people of the church. I longed to have her company and begged her to spend time with me. It rarely happened. In fact, it became apparent to me where my mother's loyalties were when she accompanied one of the young girls in the church whose own mother was a cripple, to a mother/daughter function at school that I did not get to attend because there was no one to accompany me.

Looking back on my mother's life, I now see how her self-esteem needs were, in part, being met by the people being served by her. She was considered a saint by hundreds of people. She was often self-effacing and self-sacrificing, very sweet to everyone who crossed her path, and also a very hard worker. My sister, one time in anger at my mother's unavailability, said, "If you want to know who's in control around here, look under the doormat." This was her way of seeing through our mother's con of martyrdom. It was such a radical thought in light of our intensely domineering father. But upon closer examination, I could see how even he was manipulated by her self-sacrificial sainthood.

I love my mother, God rest her soul. I cannot blame her for using what means she had to hang on to some measure of control. However, I have had to be very conscious about my own tendency to follow her model in sacrificing my own needs unnecessarily in the interest of everyone else's comfort in order to have control. When I first realized this tendency, it gave me the courage I needed to go against everything I had been taught and return to a full time career. I always tried to be very careful to arrange excellent childcare and to spend as much quality time with my son as possible. My work was a real balancer for my spiritual addiction. It kept my feet on the ground by forcing me to stay in the world when every cell of my body just wanted to do nothing else but explore my spirituality. Work also allowed me to exercise my mind and my talents. This boosted my self-esteem and caused me to experience myself as somewhat powerful, so that gradually my suicidal thoughts ceased. But I still had not yet filled what felt like the black hole in the middle of my being.

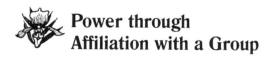
Power through Affiliation with a Group

In my starvation for power, at age thirty-two, I became active in feminist politics. This brought with it the power of affiliation. My feeling in feminist groups was not dissimilar to what a follower of Reverend Moon might have felt in one of his mass weddings. The affiliation conferred power, but it was a power that made me depend on a group's thinking instead of going inside to hear my own inner voice. To this day, I am very much in support of feminists and still consider myself a feminist. However, my affiliation with feminist groups at that point in my life was largely for the purpose of feeling powerful myself. Again, I was looking outside myself for spiritual power.

At that time, I realized how angry I was about God still being considered male by the world. So I decided to try to find a book that specifically addressed the lack of mention of *women* in history being imbued with the divine message. I went into one of the biggest and most noted bookstores in Denver thinking surely there must have been something written on the issue. I found the same old books about women in the Bible, mostly in subservient roles. I became angry with the white male store manager and turned to stomp out of the bookstore saying, "I guess I'll have to write it myself!" He called after me saying, "There's a book that came in just the other day. I don't know if it's what you're looking for. It's over there in the corner on the bottom shelf." It turned out to be exactly what I was looking for.

Just two weeks later, I was at a sales seminar. A facilitator made some reference to two of the men in our group who had apparent negative assumptions about women from the way they had spoken earlier. I was drawn to her, so I asked her to have a drink with me afterward. I told her about the book I was reading and she pulled a brochure out of her pocket, saying, "The author of your book is my therapist, and this is a brochure advertising her upcoming intensive on an island in Minnesota." I had been so moved by the book. The book spoke about the unique female system in a white male world, and the "original sin of being born female" in America. I thought that perhaps I had finally found a therapist who could help me fill the black hole. I called the number on the brochure the next day. The intensive was two weeks away, but it was full. I put myself on the waiting list.

Two days before the intensive, I was cleared from the waiting list. I was thrilled and scared. The "thrilled" feeling got me there. The "scared" feeling caused some interesting logistical obstacles to occur which had to be overcome in order to get there.

I was still scared midway through the intensive. On some level, I must have known that the new way of thinking was going to put me through some changes. I was so scared that I would have left, but I was told I would have to row the canoe from the island to the mainland by myself because no one wanted to take me back. I was too frightened to do this alone. So I stayed and had a real breakthrough emotionally. I came out of denial about how unsatisfied I was in my marriage, and I began having incest memories. The scales fell off my eyes like lead sheets—with a heavy thud!

After the intensive, I had a very difficult re-entry time back to mothering and my fast-paced job. I had spent nine days deep in process. But my experience was the beginning of developing a healthy relationship to power. I was beginning to trust my own inner knowing. I realized the importance of accepting my own unique spirituality, my worth, and my pain in a way I never could have imagined possible.

It was in the power of this group and its shared philosophy that I found the courage to divorce my husband. I would never have had the courage to do this on my own. In the meantime, I went to more intensives and worked on my growth and healing in the process community. I was Twelve Stepped into Workaholic's Anonymous by one of the process facilitators. Again, I would never have had the courage to do something as radical as a Twelve Step program. When I was a child my father would drive past the Alcoholics Anonymous meeting place and say disgustingly under his breath, "They're all atheists!" This was because the AA groups did not promote a belief in Jesus.

Through my affiliation with the process community, I found a sense of belonging that had been missing in my family. I also found, in the power of the group, the courage I needed to make some dramatic changes in my life. Deep process was a type of healing I had never experienced before. It involved totally letting go into my emotions to the point of really losing control and experiencing what we call insanity. Each time I did this, to my amazement, I returned to greater sanity.

A few years later, as I was getting ready to attend an intensive in southern Colorado, I had a very strange feeling of uneasiness. But I had written a song about my experiences in the process community and I was very excited to share it with the group. So I was determined to go. I decided that the uneasiness was fear about some learning I would accomplish in the upcoming intensive. I pushed past the feeling, certain that, with the group's help, I could handle whatever needed to be processed. When I arrived, I soon discovered the less-than-comfortable sleeping quarters assigned to me at the lodge. I was also disappointed to learn that a particular man was participating who was sexually attracted to me. He was in such heavy pursuit mode that I had been having difficulty getting him to honor my boundaries. I thought that these things were what my uneasiness was about. Then, at one point during the intensive, I sang the song I had written, and the response from the founder was very nonchalant. I noticed that no one else was going to say anything about the song in her presence. I was very disappointed about this. It triggered all my old psychological baggage about not belonging.

One evening, during a group session, the founder unjustly, in my opinion, accused one of the participants of caressing her leg in the group session to attract the founder's boyfriend. I just could not believe it. So I spoke up, saying that I felt it was important to trust the participant's word that, in fact, she had no intentions of seducing anyone by rubbing her leg. I was told very bluntly by the founder at that point that I was codependently trying to rescue the facilitator in front of the group. I said that it did not feel like I was being codependent but that I was only interested in the truth being told. I instantly felt a heavy energy of disapproval from the other forty-some people in the room. I realized that I was questioning the founder's perception of things and that this was a very unpopular thing to do. So I let go of the discussion immediately. But I noticed how uncertain I became about my perceptions of the incident and how I doubted my own intuitive understanding.

That night I had a dream. Even though I was staying in a lodge, in the dream, I was in my down sleeping bag under the stars. All of a sudden, the Earth started trembling as if there was an earthquake. I became very frightened. Then I noticed a giant lion coming from the edge of the woods toward me. He was so huge and walked with such force that every time he put a foot down, the Earth shook. I was paralyzed in fear. At that time in my life, I had sworn off any idea of God, so I prayed in desperation to my spirit guides for help. The lion came right up to me, bent down over my head, and said some words in my ear loudly and angrily, in a language I could not understand. Then he walked back toward the woods. I asked my guides what he had said. They told me that he had said, " Don't ever do anything without checking in with the lion first!"

I did not initially understand the dream. Over the next few months, however, I realized that the dream was telling me that there was no reason to look outside myself for answers. I realized that I had become dependent on the "deep process" group for my understanding, perceptions, and direction in life and that the lion (my spirit) was very angry about this. Incidentally, my astrological sign is Leo, the symbol for which is the lion.

Eventually, I came to discover more "cultish" aspects of the group. There was an implication in the group intensives that "deep process" was "the only way" to heal and be in the world. The process community had an "us and them" perspective. The participants believed that they lived "in process" while the rest of the world behaved out of an addictive pathology. As in all cults, participants were discouraged from socializing with anyone who didn't live "in process" (according to their beliefs). While the group promoted total inclusion of all emotional states, it excluded all other belief systems. This exclusivity promoted isolation from the mainstream.

Even though the mainstream world is fraught with problems of violence and addiction, and a myriad of other social ills, its diversity is its checks and balances. Without diversity, groups become incestuous and ingrown.

There was also frequent mention in the group of "being hit upside the head with a two-by-four." This was the founder's metaphor for implying that our skulls were so thick that we could not understand without being smacked. It was useful to her in making sure that we felt inferior to her great wisdom and became solidly dependent on her. I never liked this kind of language, even from the beginning. It reminded me too much of my childhood abuse.

Years later, after doing a weekend workshop with Thich Nhat Hanh, I decided that I wanted a teacher like him rather than one who used what I felt was abusive and controlling language. Even though I was still addictively looking outside myself for the perfect teacher, I was beginning to shift from one who was abusive and controlling to one who embodied peace.

In the process group, the serious legal question of

sexual impropriety on the part of the founder was an enormous red flag. There were serious legal questions being debated in courts of law with respect to how process facilitators related to their clients. As I understood it, the founder claimed that she did not do therapy and therefore was not responsible for the typical things that happened between therapists and client such as sexual energy, transference, and counter-transference. In other words, she rejected the laws of the land that prohibited sexual relationships and dual relationships of any kind with clients in a therapeutic setting on the grounds that her groups were not "therapeutic settings." Consequently, the founder was sued more than once for sexual impropriety. But at the time I was attending sessions, I believed that I needed this woman's wisdom and spent a lot of money following her groups around the country.

Toxic Service

There is another kind of power that is particularly seductive to spiritual seekers. It is the power that comes from spiritual service. As a child, I was taught that only special people were called by God to service. Now I understand that every one of us is called to perform some form of service in the world. However, as a child, I knew that I would never be called because I was "the bad one" in the family. In fact, out of eight children, I was the only one who did not go into a full-time career of Christian service.

If my siblings did not attain a prominent position of leadership in the church, they married men who were ministers or who were studying to become ministers. One of my older sisters married a college professor at a Christian religious college.

When I first left home, I embarked on my quest for feelings of empowerment. I dropped out of college and joined four other twenty-year-olds to start a halfway house for teenage runaways and drug addicts. I wanted to show my family that I was worthy of being called by God to service. I also wanted to show them what I thought true Christian service was. This misunderstanding of service engendered spiritual abuse.

Our teacher was an ex-Children of God leader. David Berg, son of a radio evangelist, had started the movement in the mid-sixties. The Children of God story paralleled the David Koresh story in that it involved one man's interpretation of the Bible and many people who wanted to hear what that man had to say. At its apex, COG spanned seventy-two countries and had an estimated membership of ten thousand people. Even though our teacher, Steve, agreed with David Berg's Bible teachings, he did not like his own demeaned position in the hierarchy. So he left Berg's group and came to Indianapolis to start his own group. He taught us the revolutionary side of Christ's life, and we all became radical Christians with contempt for all other forms of organized Christianity.

We opened the halfway house in Talbot Village, the worst part of Indianapolis. In fact, my mother read a report in the newspaper about human fingers and toes being found in a murdered man's pockets in Talbot Village. Apparently, he had been walking to a sacrificial ceremony at the Satanic church, which was just four blocks away from our halfway house. However, even in this neighborhood, we left our doors unlocked and took in teenage runaways, drug addicts, and the disenfranchised in general. We were young, felt invincible, and never even thought about danger.

The house was three stories high and had seven bedrooms and two large kitchens. Many long-haired street people and some middle-class hippies came to volunteer service regularly. We created a community, and I do believe we really offered some sort of help. We collected and distributed free food and clothing to anyone who had a need.

However, I was doing this service for the wrong reasons. My parents were deeply embarrassed in their local Christian community because my friends and I called ourselves "Jesus Freaks." On some level (more subconsciously than consciously), I was happy with my parents' discomfort because I was getting revenge for all the abuse I had sustained from them. My revenge was an attempt to retrieve my lost power and exercise it over those who I perceived had taken it from me. I am sure I enjoyed this feeling on some level.

I was also doing the service to feel worthy of God. Had I been able to be honest with myself at the time, I would have recognized that I had no interest, really, in the people of that community. I was performing what Ram Dass calls "toxic service." Toxic service is service done out of an attitude of pity without recognition of the divinity in the ones being served. When toxic service is administered, those being served are left to deal with a bombardment of toxic energy. In this case, the people in the community were getting the toxic energy of the revenge, pity, condescension, and self-righteousness of those of us giving the service. Most of them were unconscious of the toxicity. All they could do was absorb it and get sicker or more off balance as a result. Our service to them was merely a temporary fix and may have been more painful for them than if we had not done anything at all. Having food and clothing temporarily just highlighted their pain at not having what they needed after we got bored with the project. Had we been able to provide authentic service, perhaps transformation for those of us identified as the servers would have occurred and the people we were serving may have been empowered and changed permanently. But we were the vampires in this situation, stealing people's chi by finding self-validation in toxic service to them when in reality we had nothing but pity for them. This was ignorance and spiritual snobbery, and it was much more harmful than it was helpful. But it did give us a sense of power.

Authentic service is when the person doing the service recognizes no distinction between themselves and the one being served. As Ram Dass says, "like taking money out of our pocket and putting it in our other pocket." When approached from this understanding, the server automatically recognizes God or consciousness in the one being served. The act of pity does not recognize the divinity of the one receiving help.

I am grateful to my guardian angels for keeping my

spirit safe all those years when I was indulging in my quest for personal power. I had some crash landings from seeking to fly without knowing how to land. I paid a very high price financially and emotionally. Until recently, I suffered deep confusion and was unable to discover my area of service or passion, my right livelihood.

The root of all seduction is the desire to know God, which is the same desire as wanting to know ourselves. We are God. One way to know that we are God, despite the fact that God seems so much bigger than ourselves, is to recognize that we are not our physical identities, our karmic incarnations. The way I see it is that each lifetime is just a blip on the radar screen: a small moment in the overall scheme of things. Our true nature is consciousness itself. It remains when our bodies fall away. We are consciousness. I believe that the antidote to spiritual vampires, whether they operate from ignorance, developmental arrestment, or aggressive maliciousness, is self-knowledge. Knowing ourselves involves abiding in the awareness that we are consciousness. One way to know ourselves is to ask the question "Who am I?" as Ramana Maharshi instructed. We need to follow the question back as far as we can push our minds. I believe it is an opportunity to experience the apparent death of our self-image as we see who we truly are. This is the healing and the end of our seducibility by spiritual vampires and of all of our suffering.

It has only been since 1991 that I have begun to live a happy, joyous and free life. When I met Gangaji in November 1991, it was the end of the search for me. What happened for me is difficult to put into words, but I discovered that my compulsive search for personal power turned out to be the fist that had been driving me so hard all my life, my hound of heaven. It was my burning passion for freedom. I am so grateful that the search is finally over. When I realized that my true nature is consciousness itself and the source of all power, the spiritual fist in my back melted into a warm burning ember at the center of my being. This ember emanates peace and surrender to what *is* and compels me toward natural growth and deepening expansiveness.

chapter eight

Breaking Free

You know, after all is said and done
The only thing of any real interest
Is the burning passion for freedom.

I don't even concern myself anymore
When my spirit is here and my heart is over there.

It's love that gets me every time
Showing up as God in drag
Asking to love me.

THE JOURNEY TO FREEDOM from spiritual abuse is not an easy one. Those of us on this journey can be helped by seeing what other people have encountered in their healing. Their healing serves as a sort of map of the terrain. Over the course of interviewing dozens of spiritual abuse survivors, I observed five basic phases, similar to Elizabeth Kubler-Ross' stages of reconciliation with death, that people commonly experience in the course of their healing. I also noticed that they shared some common withdrawal symptoms throughout the various phases of healing. These are illustrated in the chart below. I also observed that spiritual abuse survivors do not always go through these phases in chronological order; sometimes they go back and repeat a phase. As we know, nothing is ever an exact science where human beings are concerned.

Healing Phase	Common Withdrawal Symptoms
Phase 1: Recognition	shock, terror, agoraphobia, fear of death, paranoia
Phase 2: Bargaining	depression, despair, suicidal thoughts, deep fatigue
Phase 3: Anger	suicidal thoughts, accidents and illness, terror of hurting self or others
Phase 4: Surrender	deep sadness, shame, great uncertainty but mostly relief
Phase 5: Grief	deep emotional grieving, heart opening, acceptance and surrender to the truth of what is, revelations of the internal source of truth, physical and spiritual rejuvenation

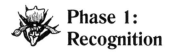 Phase 1: Recognition

The first phase is the moment of recognition that the insanity or abuse must stop. This happened for me at age fourteen when I said a prayer out loud that got me kicked out of my family. I came to the conclusion that I could no longer tolerate the insanity.

The prelude to my recognition experience started with rheumatic fever in my right knee and ankle. The pain was almost unbearable. My family put a box over my foot and leg because even the vibration of someone walking by caused excruciating pains to shoot up my leg. I should have been put on some sort of medication immediately, but my father would not allow me to be taken to a doctor, insisting that God could heal me. It was a very long time before I got well. I missed a lot of school that year. This was another example of spiritual abuse. Because of my father's religious beliefs about God and healing, I suffered a permanent injury. The heart murmur resulting from my illness could have been avoided through the use of medicine. But even so, as was so often the case for me, my illness was yet another herald of a coming transformation.

While I lay sick, unable to move, hardly able to think, I once again practiced the stillness my mother had taught me at age five. It was the only thing that controlled the pain. During the stillness, I realized I needed help if I was ever going to stop hating everyone around me. I prayed to Jesus for help.

Shortly after I was able to walk again, my family attended the annual camp meeting in Indiana. While there, I not only got help but also had an experience that moved me closer to my first moment of recognition. One Saturday morning, I was hanging around the outside of the tabernacle because I had my hair up in curlers. I had nothing to do and was somewhat interested in what the preacher was saying. The tabernacle had a roof with many steel pillars and was open on all sides except for a wall behind the pulpit platform. It was a very large tabernacle which held five thousand people. The preacher was speaking on a passage in 1st Corinthians about "the cleansing of the mind." I was in much emotional pain and was about as angry as a person could be. I understood him to say that if I could have a cleansing of my mind, I would be free of the pain of hatred and anger. I regretted that my hair was still wet because I could not take the curlers out until it dried. So I asked myself how badly I wanted a cleansing of my mind. At age fourteen, I had to want it pretty badly to put pride aside and go to the altar at the preacher's invitation, much less with my hair in curlers. But that is exactly what I did.

My mother was sitting about midway down the front of the tabernacle. She saw me head toward the altar and followed. I told her what I wanted. Several other women joined her to pray for me. She told them what I wanted. The long altar wrapped around the entire platform. From where we were on one side, much of the altar was blocked from view, which gave us a bit of privacy. My fourteen-year-old mind envisioned a vacuum sweeper going through every cell of my brain, sweeping everything up to leave it completely empty and clean. I felt totally clean, very whole and loving afterward. I was actually able to like the people around me for the first time since I was five years old. I thought to myself, "This is how it's supposed to be."

This was one of only three experiences I had during all my church-going years that I can claim as truly transformational. It was transformational because it inspired my internal vision of cleansing my mind and reconnecting to my spirit. The transformation may have had very little to do with that particular minister. I did not know him well, but I have since recognized that people can get spiritual help under any circumstances if their hearts are pure. For example, I have witnessed people be healed by religious healers who were admitted charlatans; I am sure it was the purity of their own faith that healed them. The cleansing of my mind was the preparation for my moment of recognition that the insanity had to stop.

About six weeks later, my family was getting ready to go to church. My father made a derogatory comment about my sister's and my mascara. He told us to wash it off because he did not want his daughters looking like "harlots." His voice got louder, and he began to raise his arms in violent gestures. Then he told my sister that she looked like a harlot in "that sweater." He told her to change it. When she asked why, his anger escalated even more and he began preaching about lust and lasciviousness. He eventually hit her hard across her breasts and told her never to wear sweaters again. Without thinking, I jumped between them, and he backhanded me so hard I flew back. I heard my shoulder blades crack against the ledge on the fireplace mantle behind me. As a result, I have had chronic back pain between my shoulder blades most of my adult life.

Then my father made us kneel to ask for forgiveness, as was customary in our family whenever he raged. I knew from past rage outbursts that his energy had been spent and that we had some time before his rage could build again. So I put my hands over my ears when he prayed for our forgiveness. When it was my turn to pray, instead of asking for forgiveness, I prayed out loud: "God, please send help because he is crazy." I was so desperate and angry, I did not care what he might do! I sincerely begged God to help us. This was my moment of recognition.

This incident was an example of three things: sexual abuse, spiritual incest, and ritual abuse. It was sexual abuse because my father's repressed, unmanaged sexual energy caused him to rage uncontrollably at our budding sexuality. It was spiritual incest because his spiritual beliefs, in this case about mascara and sweaters that revealed breast curves, were violently imposed on us. And it was ritual abuse because we were made to ritually kneel and ask forgiveness for causing him to get angry.

I would not have had the courage to say that prayer had I not had the transformational experience six weeks earlier at the camp meeting. Because of that experience, I felt much stronger than I had ever felt before. It did not matter what my father's reaction might be. I had had enough of the insanity!

The consequences of my prayer showed up very soon. I was in the pantry ironing the next Saturday morning. The swinging door of the pantry was the only thing between me and my parents' discussion of the incident in the next room. I heard my father say to my mother, "From now on, she's your responsibility. I want nothing to do with her. You need to find a place for her to live with one of your brothers or sisters." My heart sank! I could not breathe. My body got very hot, as if it were burning all over. My heart pounded hard with fear. I had not dreamed that the consequences of my prayer would involve being kicked out of my family.

Over a period of several months, I anxiously awaited the replies of my aunts and uncles. They were all negative. I felt abandoned. I started thinking about what I could do to find a place to live. Mother used to take the family to the dental school in Indianapolis to get our teeth fixed. I fantasized about approaching people in the city to ask them if I could go home with them. But I never had the courage to approach anyone.

After a few months, things naturally evolved. I began spending more time at my boyfriend's house and school-related events. When I was at my family's home, I was shunned by my father, and also by my siblings when they were in my father's presence. It was as if I was not there. My father still punished my siblings when they came in past curfew time, but not me. All of his parenting of me stopped. This was scary for me, but the emotional distance allowed me to develop a more objective view of my family and the church. I decided that I would never make it in their religion. I gave up trying to do it right. I chose to simply take my chances on hell not being so bad. I continued to go to church because there really was no choice about this in my family or my boyfriend's family. This moment of recognition may have brought painful consequences, but the benefit was that it was the last time my father physically or sexually abused me, and it was the first step in my long journey of healing from spiritual abuse.

As an adult, through my work, I have been able to help others come to their moments of recognition. I present a storytelling class to adults who use it as a healing medium. The class is based on the twelve-phase healing center called Epidaurus in Asclepius, in ancient Greece (500 B.C. to 600 A.D.). The ancient center's philosophy did not distinguish between physical, emotional, and spiritual illness. Any illness was considered to be a malfunction of a person's essential nature. The participants in the Epidaurus program did not have to feed themselves or contribute to society on any level. The community brought food to the center each day. Upon entry, participants were asked to commit to the whole program, which included nutrition, mineral baths, hikes, body work, and daily exercises. They did not graduate from one stage to the next until the entire community of staff and participants unanimously agreed on their readiness. Each individual healed at his or her own pace. During the twelfth and last stage, the participants went to sleep in the dreaming caves until they had a dream of significance. If they did not understand the message of the dream, they could take it to a priest or priestess for interpretation. Once their dream was interpreted, they performed it in an amphitheater before a carefully selected audience. Usually, the audience consisted of the staff and other participants plus a few trusted and "safe" family members.

The quote that I use on my promotional literature is from C. S. Lewis' novel, *Till We Have Faces*: "And when that time comes when you say the thing that has lain at the center of your soul, which you have been thinking over and over, idiot like, you will say the very thing that you mean, nothing more, nothing less than what you *really* mean. And saying it is to be answered."

I love facilitating people in accessing the story that lies at their innermost core. It is such a clean process compared to most of the other healing mediums in which I have participated because there is no coddling. It is impossible for this technique to foster dependency because the story waiting to be told is only authentic when it is discovered by the storytellers themselves.

One man who wanted to transform his suicidal tendencies told a particularly profound story. Vaughn's storytelling performance was entitled "I Want Out!" As he was lying on the floor of my living room, completely covered with an afghan, he quoted Hamlet from under the blanket:

> *To die, to sleep*
> *No more—and by a sleep to say we end*
> *The heartache and the thousand natural shocks*
> *That flesh is heir to. 'Tis a consumption*
> *Devoutly to be wished. To die, to sleep...*

At this point, Vaughn stopped and pulled the blanket off his head saying, "Marty, please help me. I've been in therapy now for twenty years, Twelve Step meetings for fifteen of those twenty, and I've done every meditation workshop that my work schedule allowed for the last seven years. What is it going to take for me to move beyond this prison of pain?" Vaughn was a large, fit, attractive Italian man, and a successful therapist. His plea was so sincere and desperate, that I felt my own tears well up.

A participant's story is never completely known until the final performance. It often changes to some degree in the telling of it. One week before his performance, Vaughn changed the title of his story "Blood." During the nine-week process of uncovering the story waiting to be told at the core of his being, he had discovered the preciousness of his own psychospiritual "blood" and how he had unwittingly offered it to be bled by his "helpers" (therapists, meditation teachers, and so on), from whom he had continually sought counsel. Vaughn's story revealed to him that it was time to stop the insanity of his spiritual addiction—the compulsive search for God outside himself. This search had placed him within easy access of spiritual vampires who had bled him dry. This was the first phase of his healing from spiritual abuse—the moment of recognition that the insanity must stop.

 Phase 2: Bargaining

The second phase of healing is the bargaining phase. During this phase, we, the survivors, rationalize our continued affiliation with our spiritual abusers in order to put off our inevitable and painful departure from them. Our process illustrates Carl Jung's log cabin theory. Jung said that human beings typically grow by taking several steps forward and one back. When we outgrow our little cabin, we begin thinking about building a new cabin down the road. We very enthusiastically draw up the blueprints and put tremendous energy into the new place. Finally, the day comes when we move into our new home. When we get there, however, we realize that none of the paintings or furniture from our old place fit, and we feel very uncomfortable. We are so uncomfortable that we eventually decide to move back to the old place and rent out the new one. But when the old place cramps us again, we finally get the courage to do the inevitable move once again to the new place.

I have gone through several bargaining phases in my own healing process. The first was after the nightmarish incident at age fourteen when I resigned myself to settle for hell. But, after a year or so, I went through a period of trying even harder than ever to be a good Christian. I told myself that maybe I had spoken too quickly—that my father deserved another chance. You might ask why I did not just take my freedom and run. This eternal hope of being loved is common among abused children. I hoped against hope that my father would reconsider and love me after all. I worked hard to win the approval of church members in the hope that I could somehow win back my family. But, it was to no avail.

Years later, while presenting at a workshop on healing from spiritual abuse, I met a woman who had been sexually molested by her minister in a counseling session at her fundamentalist Christian church. Michelle was a big, beautiful woman who was very soft spoken. I had to ask her to repeat things several times so I could hear what she was saying. It was funny. At one point during the first day of the workshop, she happened to mention that she was still attending the same church. The rest of us simultaneously turned our heads toward her in astonishment. She was in the bargaining phase. She was rationalizing her continued attendance at that church, even though she had lost all faith in it.

It is hard to believe that we go back for abuse even after we have recognized the insanity of it. However, we perceive danger unconsciously before we perceive it consciously. The trusting of our own knowing is a process. It usually takes some time to fully integrate what we know *sub*consciously into our aware consciousness. This was true for Rex, whose story was told in chapter five. Rex stayed on at the spiritual community even after he realized the insanity of the leader.

 Phase 3: Anger

The third phase of healing occurs when the anger surfaces. Usually, this phase is triggered by some incident related to the source of the spiritual abuse. It is in this phase that we get the fortitude to take aggressive action and make changes.

Rex reached phase three when he attended one of his spiritual community's business meetings. He had donated several houses to the community, and when he tried to offer his ideas about how the houses should be used in light of the community's financial situation, the leader embarrassed him in front of the group. The leader said that if they relied on his financial expertise, the entire community would be out on the streets tomorrow. This was the incident that sent Rex over the edge. He had given so much of his own property to the community that his own financial future was desperately at stake. Later, when he told the story to me, he said, "I looked at the leader at that moment and I saw his ugliness. All I could think of was how he's never seen without a bottle of Jack Daniels and a pretty little woman hanging around him. I was so angry, I actually felt sick to my stomach." Rex left the group permanently after this incident.

Phase 4: Surrender

The fourth phase of healing is the phase of final surrender. This is the beginning of the death of the bond with the group, the philosophy, or the teacher. When Rene, the Mormon bishop's daughter, showed up six months after I had initially interviewed her at a workshop on healing from spiritual abuse, I experienced her very differently. She had moved through the first, second, and third phases of healing and had reached the fourth phase of surrender. When I asked her how her three children were doing with the move away from her family and the church, she named numerous problems. Then she said, "You know, I'm realizing that most of our problems come from the fact that I've never bonded with any of my children. I was told to have them for the church." She had started therapy to heal her deep resentment at having three unwanted children. She had also found a doctor who combined Western medicine with alternative medicine to address the physical illnesses associated with her reproductive organs. She felt that these illnesses were due to having three souls come through her body who were not consciously invited.

Rene shared some of her progress around this healing with me. She laughed and said, "The children and I are figuring out how to live with each other. I'm a very different mother these days than I have ever been before. They're learning to accept the fact that I'm never going to be a typical mother. Do you remember the instruction the flight attendant gives you to put your own oxygen mask on first and then help your kids? This is the kind of mother I am now. I can't say it's all a piece of cake, but it's working." This was my clue that Rene's philosophic and emotional bonds with the Mormon church had died. She had finally surrendered to the cards that life had dealt her. She had come home to herself.

 **Phase 5: Grief**

Rene moved right into the fifth phase of healing during the workshop. As she sobbed in deep grief, I noticed her natural beauty replace the hard tension in her face. Grief,

grief, sweet relief!

When grieving is done fully and consciously, survivors can release themselves from the psychological conditioning that drew them to their spiritual abusers in the first place. The healing elements of grief are tremendous and almost magical. I heard David Steindl-Rast, a Christian monk, speak about grief once. He said genuine grieving, which most of us go to great lengths to avoid, is the aerobics for the spiritual heart muscle. Grieving the losses in our lives strengthens our hearts. This causes our hearts to open—to the love of others, and to the acceptance of ourselves and our own lives. Elizabeth Kubler-Ross, in her death-and-dying workshops, talks about the value of grieving our losses. She says that grieving changes us at the cellular level so that all slates (our programming or conditioning) are cleaned which allows us a brand new start. When we have clean slates, profound changes in our lives are not only possible, but inevitable.

 **Complete Healing**

All five phases are essential for the complete healing of spiritual abuse wounds. I was privileged to witness a beautiful gay man go through all the phases before he died. Randy had AIDS at the time I met him. He had been assigned to me by the Living and Dying Project upon completion of my facilitator training. When I shared my vision of writing this book, he asked if I would include his story.

Soon after we met, Randy discovered that we shared a common background in Twelve Step programs. He was anxious to make sure that I knew he was no longer a Twelve Stepper. He angrily told me, "All Twelve Step groups consist of self-centered, arrogant victims!" He had been in Alcoholics Anonymous for several years and had been successful in staying away from alcohol. But he first became disenchanted with the Twelve Steps when he tried to share his realizations of his own Godness in the meetings. He was actually ridiculed by the other AA attendees who declared that they would be drinking tomorrow if they began thinking they were God. Randy had come from a fundamentalist Baptist background and was very anti-church, but he felt a deep need to be around people who were claiming their own Godhood. He said that the concept of a God "out there" was a dangerous concept for him spiritually. However, he was solidly dependent on AA because he was afraid he would start drinking again. So he continued in AA and said very little in the meetings.

About a year prior to my meeting Randy, he began attending Sex and Love Addicts Anonymous (SLAA). He had difficulty at first because the stories that were shared at a particular gay mens' meeting were so graphic that he had even more trouble abstaining from acting out his sexual fantasies on the streets. Also, the meetings were somewhat of a "meat market" in that a fair number of men, according to Randy, were there to pick others up. In fact, he was "hit" on several times himself. He was quite desperate for help but realized he could not afford to expose himself to this kind of trigger for his addiction. He was terrified to quit and terrified to continue attending the meetings. This kind of helpless terror is common among survivors in the first phase of healing from spiritual abuse.

Randy did quit for three months, but he realized his desperate need for help and did not know where to turn. So he resumed the SLAA meetings but attended different ones and told himself he would get the help of a sponsor this time. With this action, he entered the bargaining phase of healing. He chose a sponsor who at first seemed to have a lot of recovery and maturity. But some months later, this sponsor began questioning him about his sexual preference. Randy relied on his good nature to continue to deal with the process because he was still terrified to quit going to meetings. He had learned to get along with this kind of prejudice, mostly by ignoring it. Eventually though, the sponsor gave him the name and phone number of an "expert therapist" who had apparently been successful in "fixing" gays' heads so they could learn to be heterosexual. The conflict of their relationship, a typically intimate one between sponsor and sponsee, came to a head. It was Randy's anger in the third phase of healing from this abuse which gave him the courage to part with his sponsor and the SLAA meetings. He was at this stage when we met. He told me early on that he had decided to find a therapist whose expertise was sex addictions.

I lost touch with Randy when I moved away from San Francisco, but prior to my moving, we attended several satsangs with Gangaji during which he asked her about death. I was quite moved to watch him surrender to the illness and his inevitable death. The last time I spoke with him, his doctors were desperately trying to stop the bleeding of his gums after dental surgery. That was the only time I saw him break down in tears to grieve the loss of the years to AIDS, the sadness of not having pursued his talent for painting, and the realization that he was going to be leaving his friends soon, most of whom were dealing with AIDS themselves.

Prior to his physical degeneration from AIDS, Randy had been politically active. He had been one of the main organizers of the gay parades in San Francisco. He felt he had been spiritually abused by our culture in that his coming out was still considered an act of civil disobedience by most Americans. My heart broke as I heard him talk about the spiritual consequences he had suffered because he was gay. He said, "I was guilty simply by being alive. There was never any judge or jury. I was guilty simply because I was gay. And I consider what happened to me as a child spiritual murder. There was so much shame in my family because of my gayness that I eventually lost all sense of myself as a divine being. The shame progressed to spiritual soul murder. It was as if the world viewed me as having something wrong with my essential nature just because of my sexual preference. This lack of respect for my essential nature is a violation of my spirit. But even with all of that, it's been a good life in some ways. AIDS has caused me to stop and take a long look at myself, as it has for many people. I think that the world is shifting in its perception of gays. I've seen so many families have major heart openings because of a son or sibling who is dying of AIDS. This is the gift of AIDS for all of us, including the gay community." Having moved through all the phases of healing, Randy reached a sense of peace before he died.

Storytelling brought me to the surrender phase and was a real key in my own healing from spiritual abuse. At one point in my spiritual journey, I created a theater piece in which I performed my own story and a medicine wheel to find out what to do next. I had learned about the medicine wheel from a Navajo shaman. I was taught that, traditionally, Native Americans come together to bring their medicine—their prayers, wisdom, and so on—to a problem or person at the center of the medicine wheel. Prior to my traditional medicine wheel process, I performed my own story, told from the perspective of one of my guardian angels. I wanted to be healed from the pain of the black hole in me that would not be filled no matter what I did. In other words, I wanted healing of my spiritual addiction. I wanted to find my right livelihood and a spiritual practice that would finally give me a respite from the fist in my back.

For my medicine wheel ceremony, I chose five people in my community who I felt were spiritually grounded. I asked four of them to be the chiefs representing the four elemental directions. North represented physical power, the element of earth. East represented the mental plane, the element of air. South represented the spiritual, the element of fire. West represented the emotions, the element of water. The fifth chief was the heyoka. I asked my therapist to be the heyoka. She was dumbfounded because she had never been asked to support a client in this way, but she was honored to participate.

The way I was taught this ceremony, the heyoka is the chief who facilitates the process. Once the question is determined, it is then asked of each of the chiefs. They confer with their tribes. Their responses are given to the heyoka, who then turns the question upside down. Once again, it is responded to by each of the four groups and their respective elemental influences (four directions). The unanimous response is given to the person needing the healing after the final dance of the four chiefs and the heyoka.

The medicine wheel ritual was a beautiful ceremony held in an oceanside room at the Marin Headlands. There were about forty-two people in attendance. However, I was quite frustrated at the end when the chiefs came to me in the final ceremony to give me the answer. The answer was essentially: Relax! This medicine seemed too superficial, not nearly complex enough for my problem. But the Native Americans say that the only way to see if the medicine works is to swallow it. So I did. Amazingly, throughout the next few weeks, when I relaxed my mind, I quit searching altogether. I let go of the hope of ever filling the black hole or of ever feeling whole. This was my fourth phase of healing. I finally became willing to surrender to whatever the truth really was.

After a few weeks of truly letting go of all thoughts and actions with respect to the black hole, I began grieving. This was my last phase of healing from spiritual abuse and spiritual addiction. I allowed myself to grieve deeply. I went on a week's retreat and cried for days. The great thing about emotion is the "motion" part of it. The grieving moved me to a place of emptiness that made space for the truth to show up.

And show up, it did! One month later, my friend Alice told me about a female spiritual teacher who was visiting from Maui. I trusted Alice's judgement. Alice was the chief of the East at the medicine wheel ceremony. She had witnessed my journey through the various encounters with spiritual vampires in my life. I went to hear Gangaji in Carmel, California. It was the beginning of the end of the fist in my back. I found Gangaji to be a clear reflection of the Self. She was very attentive to the seeker's tendency to guru-ize her. She would not allow this projection. She continually pointed the seeker back to the Self. She charged no money. She said she was simply doing what she had been told to do by her master which was to invite people for tea and tell them who they really were. This was revolutionary for me. I was deeply struck by her integrity.

Gangaji's first teaching was about "surrendering to the 'yes' in each moment." She said, "Relax!" I could not help but remember the "medicine" to relax from the medicine wheel. I went to dinner with friends following that meeting. I saw "yes" on the license plate of a car. I saw "yes" in a merchant's store window all lit up in neon. When we arrived at the restaurant, there was a huge arrow with a "yes" on it pointing to the door of the women's room. It was at that point that I got it. This was the end of a long journey of searching. Yes! Yes! Yes, it was!

Looking back on the progression of events in my spiritual journey, I see them all coming full circle. There was a Sioux influence at the beginning of my life and there was the Native American tradition that assisted me in finally finding "home." The medicine to relax from the medicine wheel was what allowed me to find satsang. In satsang, which means association with truth, the first step in self-realization is to relax. In the state of relaxation, the mind stops. And it is only when the mind is quiet that we can realize the illusory nature of what we call reality. The medicine wheel facilitated my coming to the fourth phase of surrender. Upon surrendering, I began grieving the loss of the years of suffering. The truth became revealed to me through Gangaji. Because I was relaxed, I could feel the truth resonate within me. My time with Gangaji led me, and continues to lead me, to deeper and deeper levels of healing from looking outside myself and all the years of the spiritual abuse. The gift of my grieving was meeting Gangaji in November 1991.

Since that time, I have witnessed the fist in my back melt into a warm burning ember. This ember emanates in all directions from the center of my being. The teachings of Ramana Maharshi are now clear. I know now that my true nature is happiness. Identifying with myself solely as Marty Raphael, the limited karmic incarnation, is the cause of all my suffering. I have come to learn that I am really, consciousness itself. I know that I am not separated from anything or anyone. Suffering is a thing of the past. This is not to say there is no pain or growth yet to be experienced in my life. But I experience much less psychological suffering, mental negativity and need for control. The normal pains of being human are still a reality, but they are curiously pleasurable when directly experienced without resistance. I experience them with the feeling that there is always an "open window," a spaciousness or flowing movement. I have a feeling of aliveness and well being, the same as when I experience joy and bliss.

chapter nine

Life without Vampires

She's Flying

She's flying
And no one sees her up there.
They see her on the ground.
She's smiling
Because she knows she's up there
Flying like a clown.
She's laughing because it tickles;
Feels like golden rain.
She's laughing because it tickles;
She's forgotten her name.

She's flying.
She looks ahead and sees
The sun and the moon.

She's flying.
She reaches out to grasp a sunbeam in her hand.
The sunbeam danced all around her
And a moonbeam joined in.
She's laughing because she's flying.
She flies; she flies. She has no wings.

She's flying
And soaring through the air
With both feet on the ground.
She's laughing.
She wonders where is up
If there is no down.
Could this be so?
It must be so.

She's singing
Because she's flying high.
The music is her breath.
It sparkles, like stars come out to greet
And welcome her home.
Could this be home?
It must be home.

After moving through the withdrawal symptoms and the healing phases from having been sexually, emotionally, mentally, financially, and physically abused by spiritual teachers, I began to experience myself and the world very differently. I began to find out what life without vampires was like.

Why were the vampires being repelled? After the completion of the last phase (deep grief), I was empty enough to really hear my own self speaking to me. And even though Gangaji was the vehicle through which I could finally hear my own voice, it wasn't only through Gangaji. I began to see Self in everything and everyone. When I had a deep realization that Self was also truth and that the truth inside myself is enough, vampires stopped showing up. As it says in the poem at the beginning of Chapter Two:

*I waited and waited expecting black blood to run down the
Pearl blue sky any minute like it used to when they were
 coming.
But it never happened. Nothing ever again happened like that.
So I got up and left.*

My work associates and friends noticed a change. They asked me: "What has happened to you? You seem so quiet and different somehow." I felt different too, but didn't know how to answer them. One very profound difference was that I was free of spiritual anxiety for the first time in my life. It was finally the end of the search. I had a pervasive feeling of enormous relief that lasted for months. I did not even know what I was relieved about.

I have always been very verbal, but at that time, I could hardly speak at all, much less speak with clarity about what had happened. I simply did not have words to describe how different I felt. So when my friends asked what had happened, I told them that I did not know. In fact, I was so disoriented initially, I felt as though I didn't know much of anything at all. Everything, including the road to the grocery store, felt new. I had never relished the state of not being right on top of things, but at this point, somehow it seemed alright to not be in control.

Of course, I asked myself what had happened too. The answer came a few months later in a very small propeller plane on a business trip from Philadelphia to New York City in January 1992. The cabin was so cramped that there was hardly room for our heads. The song that opens this chapter, "She's Flying" came to me while I was hunched over in this tiny plane. It was the vision I needed to integrate my new wholeness. I sang it to one of my closest friends and her response was, "Oh, so you finally reached the place where you don't have to struggle to improve yourself anymore. I knew you'd relax someday." I resolved to sing the song to the next person who asked what had happened to me.

One day, one of my friends asked how I could be so certain that Gangaji was different from the other spiritual teachers I had experienced. She said, "She looks the same as the others. She's American-born, did all the New Age workshops and meditation groups, and was an acupuncturist and workshop leader.

One way that Gangaji was different was that she was willing to generously share information with people free of charge. When people asked why, she said she loved watching people wake up. Aside from that, she said she was simply doing what Poonjaji had asked her to do. She had never planned to hold satsangs around the world.

Gangaji's presence was the stimulus for my awakening. She was the first spiritual teacher who was an undistorted reflection of the truth inside myself. When I attempted to attribute my newfound wisdom to Gangaji, she gently but firmly pointed me back to my Self as the source of all wisdom and reminded me that she and I were not separate. I watched when others repeatedly attempted to project a "teacher" trip on her; she fiercely denied that she was a teacher or that they were students. She consistently led us back to the Self by encouraging us to ask the question "Who am I?"

The question "Who am I?" began having a profound effect on me. I had vivid and deep healing dreams that did not even seem like dreams at all. In August 1992, I dreamed that I was on one side of the Ganges and that Poonjaji was beckoning to me with open arms from the opposite side. I wondered how I was going to get across the river. Then suddenly I was across. But Poonjaji was standing behind a large gate about fifteen-feet long. I proceeded toward the slightly opened end of the gate, but as soon as I took a step to go through it, the gate closed. Then the other end of the gate opened. So I headed toward this other end, and when I was about to step through the gate again, it closed, and the original opening appeared at the other end. I noticed Poonjaji laughing uproariously behind the gate. Then I saw that there was no fence on either side of the gate, so I could have gone around the end of it at any time. I began laughing with Poonjaji in the dream, and we embraced.

After this dream, I had a deep longing to meet Poonjaji in person. I did not feel that I *needed* to see him. Instead, it was an intense feeling like that of wanting to see a friend after a long absence.

I was able to arrange a trip to India in December 1992. The first morning I was to attend satsang with Poonjaji, I told my travelling companions that they should not expect me to be devotional like the other people around Poonjaji. I said that as far as I was concerned, I was finished with devotional feelings in this lifetime. I felt mostly disgust with the appearance of the devotee "scene" around Poonjaji. Part of this scene involved a group of long-time devotees making daily decisions about who got to sit near or see Poonjaji privately.

The first satsang was an hour and a half of deep laughter for me. Poonjaji's bliss was so contagious. The satsang itself was spiritually filling enough, but when I was invited to the small room where he was welcoming approximately ten other new arrivals, I realized there was a lot more in store. Poonjaji greeted me, commenting, "You've been here before, right?" Concerned that I was not going to get to stay with the new arrivals in this intimate setting, I quickly answered that this was my first time. He looked puzzled. I asked him if I could tell him about the dream I had of him in August.

When I told Poonjaji the dream, he looked at Yamuna, his attendant, and said, "That's where I've seen her. Remember a few months ago when I told you about the woman who was having difficulty getting through the gate? Here she is!" Yamuna concurred with him that I fit the exact description of the woman he had seen. Poonjaji then smiled the brightest, sweetest smile, looked straight into my eyes, and said, "Why do you call it a dream? It was a meeting." Everyone laughed, and I noticed that I was experiencing devotion at that moment. It was not what I thought it would be. It was not like the clingy loyalty I had felt with many of the other spiritual teachers. I did not think I was bowing down to him. However, one of the other attendees later told me that I had physically bowed and placed my forehead on the ground in front of Poonjaji. All I could remember was his eruptive and contagious laughter. When I was with Poonjaji, I lost my sense of the physical world altogether. I could not feel the boundaries of my physical body. Now I understand that my Self was bowing down to my Self. There was no separation or hierarchy, just a deep feeling of love and oneness.

I was so deeply affected by this experience that I could not get my grounding when I left that little meeting room. The sky seemed to be moving in circles. I could barely feel my feet on the ground, and I was very disoriented with respect to which direction I needed to go. I knew I needed to get some food in my system to bring me back to earth. So I hired a rickshaw driver to take me to the restaurant where my friends had arranged to meet for lunch. When I arrived, the first thing they said was that I was glowing radiantly. They asked what had happened. I said, "I think I just experienced true devotion for the first time in my life, and it wasn't what I thought it would be at all." They laughed.

That night I could hardly sleep. I was so excited from

the events of the day. But as I finally drifted off to sleep, I vowed to ask Poonjaji what a healthy relationship between a guru and student would look like. The next day, someone asked him if the satsang meeting hall in Lucknow was his ashram. Poonjaji responded fiercely, "This is not an ashram. This is an airport. You fly here on a plane. You stay awhile. And then you leave on a plane! You can stay long enough to wake up and then you must follow your own inner voice. If you need me for a long time, you haven't heard me at all. I am your inner voice. My inner voice is you: the I that is we. How could we ever be separate?"

I understood from this response that there is no student and there is no guru. The beauty I saw in Gangaji and Poonjaji was the long-sought-after, undistorted reflection of the truth in my Self. We are all this truth.

There are parallels between the growth of human beings and the development of spiritual initiates. Like children who are never weaned from their mothers' breasts, devotees who hang around awakened beings only to remain in a perpetual state of bliss display a sort of spiritual immaturity. They miss the opportunity to connect with their own inner authority, which is the source of bliss, grace, and compassion.

Unfortunately, this was my experience of some of Poonjaji's followers. I heard Poonjaji ask them repeatedly, "What do you really want? Do you want bliss, or do you want to wake up?" I was quite shocked to witness how this spiritual immaturity manifested in some of the people around Poonjaji. One time I was embarrassed by one of the men who was speaking abusively to an Indian travel agent. He was using a very "power-over" kind of physical posture, punctuated by abusive language. He told the travel agent that if he could not guarantee him the lowest fares, he would send all the satsang people, which was 250 to 500 people, to the travel agent's competitor down the street. When I questioned why he had to be so forceful, he told me how stupid the Indians were. I observed this racial prejudice more often than I liked to admit while I was there.

Over the last few years, I have observed that people who claim to be awake sometimes lack the purification that comes from everyday psychospiritual hygiene. This hygiene involves necessary psychological routines to stay clear with life around us. Good psychological health is part of being grounded on the Earth and must be blended with our spirituality. We have no business living on multiple dimensions if we cannot handle the Earth plane. If we are still operating from our wounds that hide out in our subconscious, we are not able to manage the additional responsibility that automatically comes with expanded consciousness and spiritual power.

Being awake does not necessarily mean that we always act perfectly. Waking up is not about perfection. Ramana Maharshi says that when we wake up, we are perfect in our imperfection. This does not mean that we never again make a mistake. However, when we abide in the awareness of who we really are, which is, consciousness itself, we naturally want to take responsibility for all our mistakes.

While I was in India, I had some experiences that took me through some maturing processes. I had some very strong reactions to what I experienced at the time as a hierarchical pecking order around Poonjaji. At one point, the group arranged a talent show for the Christmas celebration, and I really wanted to sing my song, "She's Flying." After auditioning, I was not chosen to sing the song, and I was very disappointed. This triggered some ugly junior-high feelings of being left out of the "in" crowd. I carried these negative feelings around for several days, trying to manage them as I had learned from Gangaji. I knew that these feelings were very old and were simply surfacing to be liberated, like all demons. But even with this awareness, the pain of feeling left out did not pass. Then I had a beautiful experience.

Spiritual Heart Attack in India

I woke up one morning while it was still very dark outside. My bed was shaking. The walls were also shaking, and I realized that I needed to get out of the room since it was built entirely of cinder blocks. India was having an earthquake, and I feared I would be buried alive. Half awake and half asleep, I went out to the courtyard beside my room, but I was almost paralyzed. I could hardly move. I regressed to a young age from the fear, and crawled out crying, "Mama, mama, help me!" An amazingly beautiful Indian woman extended her hand to me, and we left. She took me to a lush green place in the country where Nelson Mandela was on retreat. He looked at me with warm eyes and a smile and said, "Marty, India is not having an earthquake. You are having a mystical experience."

Then I was back in my bed, and the quaking became even more violent. I noticed that the acute pain on the right side of my chest at heart level was so deep that it was causing the bed and the room to shake. I tried to turn over, thinking I would get some relief if I lay in a different position. But I could not move. I cried out, "Ramana Maharshi, Poonjaji, help!" Then I was able to move. As I turned over, my body left a wake of liquid light in the darkness. It was beautiful, and it felt good to finally move. So I turned over again. And again, my body left swirls of liquid light in the darkness. However, the pain did not let up at all. I lay very still, realizing in my waking state that I was not experiencing an ordinary dream. Desperately trying to manage the fearful thoughts, I asked "Who am I?" and followed that inquiry until I experienced simply being. I had no thoughts, no feelings, nothing. The pain was still very intense on the right side of my chest. But I was able to notice it without being distracted by it.

When I woke up some hours later, the pain in my chest was still very acute. I felt I should see a doctor. I was aware of my heart murmur from the rheumatic fever at age thirteen, plus I was afraid I was a genetic candidate for a heart attack since my father had had several. I was still so weak I could not move very well. My friend, Alice who was staying in the next room, brought food and water and summoned the rickshaw driver to take me to Poonjaji's house. I knew Yamuna was a doctor, but I did not discover until I arrived there that she was a cardiologist. I thought, "How synchronous!" She examined me, looked in my eyes, and said, "Marty, you're not having a heart attack. You're having a mystical experience." I flashed on Nelson Mandela's face and remembered his reassuring words: "Marty, India is not having an earthquake. You are having a mystical experience." Then I began to relax.

I went in to the next room to see Poonjaji. He asked me to tell him what had happened. He very lovingly said, "Everything quakes, and all form shakes at the sight of such beauty!" His Indian friend, who was also a medical doctor, was visiting him that day. When Poonjaji told him in Hindi what had happened to me, they both laughed out loud. Even though I did not understand what he said in Hindi, my whole body deeply relaxed. Something about their laughter put me at total ease. I knew then that the shaking was truly a mystical experience and not a physical heart attack. Poonjaji told me that the spiritual heart is on the right side and that what I had was a spiritual heart attack. He laughed, saying, "Your broken heart has cracked open." I told him that I had prayed to him and Ramana Maharshi for help in the midst of my fear. I also said that I had not prayed for many years because I had been afraid of reinforcing the idea of a God outside me. He said, "Prayer is simply consciousness asking itself for help. It's okay to pray." Tears began streaming down my face. I was crying out of sheer relief that I could pray once again without fear.

The pain on my right side decreased as the days went

by. I noticed how different my heart felt. I was in love with everything and everyone. I was even in love with the pigs in the street. I could no longer harbor any feelings of resentment toward anyone. In fact, I could not even remember my resentment or hurt feelings about being left out of the talent show. I began to recognize what a service the people at the satsang hall offered to Poonjaji and to those of us who came and went over the years.

Many people commented on my beauty. I was not accustomed to getting those kinds of comments. I never imagined myself to be physically beautiful. But after this experience, many people from satsang went out of their way to comment on my physical beauty. I fell in love with a man from Sicily. Neither he nor I could speak each other's language. We just gazed into each other's eyes and tried to speak. We mostly laughed in bliss.

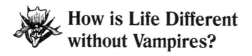 How is Life Different without Vampires?

When I returned to the United States, my enormous heart opening brought about many more changes in my maturity. Many things in my life that had not been aligned with the energy of love and surrender fell away. Many of my daily habits changed quite naturally. I stopped eating meat altogether. My bouts of depression became a thing of the past. Over a period of several months, I lost thirty pounds without even trying. I also lost the ability and tendency to work beyond my physical capabilities. I had recovered to a large degree from workaholism during the previous five years, but the miracle now was that I no longer had to be vigilant about my work habits. Since I daily asked that consciousness live me and breathe me, my tendency to work excessively fell away naturally. Paradoxically, I became much more effective in my work. I began recognizing that when I flowed with the process of specific tasks, instead of *making decisions*, I *discovered* the way to go.

Other big changes occurred very quickly. Within about six months, I met my lifetime partner. We honeymooned in the Dominican Republic for ten days to get to know each other, and I quit my corporate job in San Francisco six months later to focus full-time on writing.

Although I was experiencing a happiness unlike any I had ever imagined, I was aware of an underlying discomfort with the knowledge that there were many children still spiritually searching in similarly miserable circumstances to mine as a child. I knew from my own childhood that children naturally have a burning passion for freedom that is repeatedly extinguished by misguided spiritual helpers and adults who need to dominate and control. I felt helpless to know where to turn for a model of raising children so that they were naturally immune to spiritual vampires. Then I remembered a PBS program I had seen a couple years before, "Bali, The Last True Paradise." It had stirred me deeply to realize that there may still be a place on the planet where culture, sexuality, and spirituality were beautifully balanced and where the spirituality of children was so honored. I vowed to go to Bali and see for myself. And I did. There, I discovered their secrets!

Bali, The Last True Paradise: A Model for Gardening the Souls of our Children

Bali is an enlightened country. It is the closest thing to a vampire-free country that I have ever seen or heard about. The hearts of the Balinese people are wide open. Everywhere I went in Bali, without exception, I saw happy people. Their smiles were genuine and welcoming. It was easy to make deeply felt connections. I felt so loved!

I took as many photos of the children as I could without being too intrusive. The babies were so compelling to me. I wanted to interact with each of them. They radiated love. The Balinese believe that infants are closer to the "other side" than adults. In an effort to preserve this connection, a baby is held by an adult to keep the baby's feet from touching the ground for the first year of life. Nor do the adults allow anyone to touch the top of the infant's head, for the crown is believed to be the point of entrance for the chi or life energy. Babies are revered as divine beings or teachers who have come to the adults from the mnemonic world.

Sometimes children are not given names until they are as old as three or four years. The parents watch the children for clues to what names are fitting for the behavior, interests, and curiosities they manifest during their first few years. This is an incredible example of spiritual attentiveness from their primary caretakers. Not only do the children grow up with a core sense of value and purpose in the family and community, but they also develop a strong sense of themselves at an early age. What a beginning! Perhaps if we all had such beginnings, we would not only *not* be attracted to spiritual vampires, we would repel them because we would be so full of love and light. Just as the mythical vampires abhor light, spiritual vampires do not prey on the strong people, the ones filled with love and light.

I talked with several Balinese adults about their childhood years. I asked them if they had ever been abused by their parents or authority figures. More frequently than not, their response was blank stares. Inevitably, they would ask me what I meant by "abuse." The only story I heard that could be construed as abuse was from a tour driver who as a child was being babysat by his older brother. Katut kept running away, and his older brother had to go after him each time. So his brother tied him up to a tree. Katut cried and cried, but his brother would not untie him. When his mother returned from the market, she untied him and told the older son that he had to apologize to Katut. She also told him he could never babysit his brother again. Katut ended the story by saying that he and his brother laugh about the incident to this day.

I came from an extremely punitive family and educational background, so I could not quite believe this culture's benevolence. I researched a little further. I found a German psychotherapist who had recently terminated her therapeutic practice in Bali. She looked at me and laughed when I asked her about abuse in the Balinese culture. She said, "There is no misery here. The only time the Balinese came to see me was when they got rich too fast from tourism. When this happened, their place in the community changed, and it disrupted things for them. In fact, I no longer practice therapy. I've begun to study the healing properties of Balinese dance so that I can take this information back to Germany. This is where my heart is now. I've learned that I don't have much to teach the Balinese, and that I have much to learn from them."

The psychotherapist told me that she had attended a special "touch institute" in Germany for her graduate work. She understood only years later in Bali what she had been taught at the institute with respect to touch. She mentioned the phenomenon of the Balinese babies being held without being put down during their first year. She said that studies with German and American babies demonstrated that this kind of constant touch allows babies to advance and develop three to four times faster than average.

One day I was walking back to my bungalow from the beach, and one of the workers at a large sea resort smiled and waved. I walked over to talk to him. After a few minutes of pleasantries, I asked him how everyone in Bali could be so happy. He laughed and said, "You wouldn't come and visit us if we weren't happy, right?" Then he leaned toward me slightly and said, "We try not to think too much." I pressed for more information about how the Balinese solve their problems. He said that they wait for revelations to come through ceremonies, dreams, the words of strangers, or unusual signs in nature. If they cannot understand their dreams or the signs in nature, they go to the temple priests. He said, "When we think too much, we see many demons. The demons like thinking activity because we leave our bodies when we think and they can come right in." The Balinese use trance and dance in elaborate festivities to go into altered states. They fully expect that any questions they may have prior to commencing a dance will naturally be answered for them upon completion of the ceremony.

I think that the biggest reason the country of Bali works as well as it does is that all the people's basic needs are met within the structure of their society. This is why the Balinese are such beautiful people. For example, they have what they call banjars, which are like the townships of U.S. colonial days. A banjar is the local village council, the community extension of the house and family, and the local political unit. Every citizen of the country belongs to a banjar. And each citizen contributes a certain number of hours of labor each month to community projects such as road repair, irrigation or festival preparation. When the membership of a banjar gets too large, it is split into two banjars so that each member knows every other member personally. The Balinese believe the system only works when people know each other.

The Balinese are a very simple and humble people. They all seem to live happily with the belief that they are servants to the whole. That is to say, their individual or personal lives come second to the life of their community. But why not? Their basic needs are met in the context of their community. This sounds almost too good to be true, but then, most of us think "paradise" is beyond our everyday experience of things. However, Bali qualifies as a true paradise. And it exists on our planet!

When I speak about children being facilitated in their spiritual growth, I often use the phrase "gardening the souls of our children." This implies a natural nurturance and allowance of growth, rather than an imposed expectation based on the parents' past experience or spiritual upbringing. When we plant seeds, we watch for the growth of plants, but we do not pull on plants to make them grow. We let plants follow their own course and pace of growth. The same should be true with children. An environment of spacious allowance is the most effective environment for nurturing the spiritual growth of our children. This spacious allowance informs us quite naturally how to facilitate our children's spirituality. If we are churchgoers, we may discover that some of our children do not thrive spiritually in formal religious settings. They may need to have the freedom to explore their spirituality in nature or strictly on their own. Other children may need and desire formal religious training.

How do we "garden the souls of our children"? One of the most important ways is to prepare the ground before the seed is planted. This prepared ground is the community. A rich community supports the parents by claiming a measure of responsibility for the nurturing of the children. Children do not need to demand attention through negative means when their needs are met through family and community. When the children's divine energy expresses itself, it is important for us as adults not to squelch it out of fear of losing control of the children. We need to revere the children's spiritual growth and allow ourselves to be taught by it. Children are fed and rejuvenated by this response from their caretakers and elders.

My experience in Bali helped me get the last piece to my vision of how children can be raised so that they are not easily seduced by spiritual vampires. Before Bali, I could not see a way for community to work. It seemed that every spiritual community I ever participated in, no matter how utopian its vision, was off balance, with respect to spirituality, sexuality, or creativity. Bali is an example of a country in which people live beautifully in community. And it works.

When I returned home from Bali, I felt more peace than ever. I knew there was at least one place on the planet where life was still sane and children could grow into whole adults rather than wounded and handicapped ones. Just knowing this gave me a feeling of hope for the planet—a feeling that the planet was not completely soiled.

I attended a satsang with Gangaji later that summer. In that satsang, I said that my gratitude was so big it felt like my body could not contain it. My chest was hurting. It felt so full that I feared my rib cage was going to burst. I said that I was looking for a way to do service to give back some of the joy in order to relieve my overwhelming feelings of gratitude. But so far, the only thing that was happening was that the gratitude and bliss were continuing to grow and the gifts were continuing to come. I did not know how I was going to manage this much expansiveness. I remembered myself as the sick little girl lying in bed with hepatitis at age five, wondering how she was going to manage in the world with so much hatred and if she would ever be able to love anyone, much less love *everyone*, like Jesus.

Gangaji laughed and encouraged me to allow the bursting. She said that the body cannot contain the gratitude and that the gratitude *is* an expression of service. It reminds me of one of Rabindranath Tagore's poems that I once saw printed on a restaurant menu.

> *I slept and dreamed that life was all joy,*
> *I woke and saw that life was but service,*
> *I served and discovered that service was joy.*

I have discovered that opportunities to do service present themselves very naturally if I am still enough to see them. One such opportunity was the writing of this book about spiritual abuse survivors and my vision for the children of the world.

I don't mean to say that I have nothing more to learn. Life is an ever-deepening process of awareness of the Self. Sometimes I lose sight of my true nature and get caught up in the suffering. But now, more often than not, when this happens, I am aware that I have returned to my identity solely as this karmic incarnation. I know that as long as I abide in the awareness of who I truly am, no matter how badly a situation feels, I am home. I no longer despair about what the ultimate universal truth is, or what practice might allow me to arrive "there." I know that my true nature is truth. As long as I abide in this awareness, life is an incredibly surprising and beautiful ride.

Appendices

Characteristics of Spiritual Vampires

Every healer, twelve-step sponsor, minister, therapist, priest or new age teacher is not necessarily a spiritual vampire. If a teacher has more than two or three of the following characteristics, it is an indication they may be misusing spiritual power.

1. **They seek positions of authority** such as new age teacher, metaphysical healer, twelve-step sponsor, minister, therapist, priest, cult leader.

2. **They often present themselves as an unchallengeable authority.** This means that they want you to believe they know better than you what your truth is.

3. **They enjoy having power over people** rather than with people.

4. **They often use humiliation** to exercise control over others. At the leader's bidding, the group may have laughs at the expense of an individual member.

5. **They must feel they are in control.**

6. **They sometimes believe their spiritual teachings are above the law.** For example, one teacher I know justified having sex with one of her thirteen-year-old followers for the purpose of initiating him into adulthood.

7. **They sometimes become violent or may use mental force** when others don't agree with them.

8. **They often feel unfulfilled and bored when they're in a group where they are not the leader or teacher.**

9. **They sometimes force followers to participate in rituals against their will** saying that their individual will must be broken in order for the member to be initiated into their next level of growth.

10. **They sometimes misuse their sexuality to attract followers** or their position of authority to persuade followers to engage in sexual acts for spiritual purposes.

Characteristics of Spiritual Vampire Groups

1. There is usually a **common language** spoken in order to determine who is or is not a member of the group. For example, in the group called "Light Work," members never acknowledge wrong-doing on their part. If they've made a mistake, they claim it is the dark disembodied spirits who have entered them.

2. **High pressure tactics and manipulation** are used regularly in order to control members' thoughts and actions. Sometimes members are even asked to sign a document saying they will comply with a list of "do's" and "don't's."

3. Members' spiritual progress is often linked to their successful or unsuccessful **recruitment of new members** so that every member is compelled to get involved in proselytizing for the group.

4. **Loyalty** to the group is emphasized first and foremost—sometimes so much so that members give up their families and their entire life savings to the group.

5. Spiritual Vampire groups usually **claim to be superior** to most other groups and often engage in comparisons in their proselytizing pitch.

6. These groups are usually founded and managed by domineering people who present themselves as an **unchal-**

lengeable authority. Or if they do allow being challenged, the one who challenges is often confronted, embarrassed, or humiliated in front of other group members.

7. Language is often used to promote isolation from the rest of the world. **"Us and them" language** implies that the only safe or good place to be is with the group.

Warding Off Spiritual Vampires

1. **Trust yourself above everything else.** Recognize that you have the entire truth that you need for your life within you. This does not mean that you will never ask for help. It simply means that even in the process of asking for help, you know who or what that help should look like.

2. **Discover and do your heart's passion with respect to work.** Whether or not you're doing what you love for a living, it is important to discover your purpose and begin offering it to the world in some form. This integration with the rest of the beings on the planet is one of the strongest repellants to spiritual vampires.

3. **Creativity.** Everyone is gifted with some way in which they express themselves no matter what the medium and no matter whether the world acknowledges the product that is a result of that creativity. When we are creative, we are in relationship to ourselves. This kind of quality time spent with oneself is a very strong antidote to being manipulated by others, namely spiritual vampires.

4. A good **support system** or group of friends who generally accept you whether you're emotionally down or up. A few important intimate relationships in which you can share the very core of yourself are crucial.

5. A **solid and unwavering cosmology.** Cosmology is one's general theory of the cosmos or material universe,

its parts, elements, and laws. Another way of saying it is to say it's the way one understands "the way of things" or what the Chinese call the Tao. And remember, it is okay to doubt and shift world-views as you evolve spiritually.

Questions To Ask When Choosing A Therapist

1. Can the therapist be reached during a crisis?
2. Has the therapist worked with spiritual abuse survivors before?
3. If not, how would the therapist educate himself or herself in order to be effective with you?
4. Do you feel comfortable in his or her office?
5. Does the therapist seem judgmental or critical?
6. Do you feel the therapist wants to rescue you rather than support you in doing your own healing?
7. Does the therapist act as if he or she has all the answers?
8. Does the therapist get uncomfortable when you discover the truth for yourself without his or her help?
9. Does the therapist think that sexual contact with clients is ever appropriate?
10. Does the therapist believe that children ever willingly have sex with adults?
11. What does the therapist think about touching clients? Do you feel comfortable with his or her views on touching?
12. Does the therapist make good solid eye contact with you?
13. Can you feel free to get angry with the therapist?
14. Would you like the therapist as a friend?
15. Is the therapist willing to allow *all* your questions?
16. What does your gut say? After all, your own instincts are what can be trusted. If you are with a good therapist, you will feel respected, valued, heard and understood.

How to Pick the Good Spiritual Workshops and Avoid the Bad Ones

Counselling, workshops and personal growth seminars in general don't have to be avoided for fear of exposing oneself to spiritual vampires. We must explore, experiment and risk in order to grow. The following list includes suggestions as to how to discern the safe groups and teachers from the harmful.

1. **Word of mouth** is the best way to find out about good spiritual educational programs. If someone you know had a good experience, you can determine the results by experiencing the changes in your friend and also, by virtue of knowing your friend's tastes, etc., you can decide whether it's for you or not.

2. **A good teacher is not going to foster dependence.** If the teacher eludes to the idea that you're with him/her for the long haul, notice this characteristic as a red flag. On the other hand, if the teacher's motivation is to present information as an opportunity for you to become free and perhaps even become a teacher yourself, then you know he or she is not interested in creating a dependence on him or her.

3. **True learning is a two-way energy flow.** If the teacher does not recognize openly what he or she is learning from you or your questions, etc., it is a sign that he or she is not

being totally honest and has some hidden agenda to remain in the guru seat.

4. **If the teacher looks, feels, acts bigger than life, this is a red flag.** If the teacher allows you to see their humanness or shadow side, chances are, they're not interested in your worship, awe and or dependency on them.

5. If the amount of **money** required to take the workshop is not available to you at the time, recognize that this may be a sign that it's not right for you. Stop and check inside to see if you can see what is not immediately obvious to you with respect to where the red flags are.

6. **Trust your gut at all turns.** If you feel uneasy, and unsure about the way in which a training is going, leave immediately. *You're the only one who truly knows what you need.* Trusting your own knowing is your greatest tool in repelling spiritual vampires.

Directory of Resources

Alcoholism
Look in local phone book under Alcoholics Anonymous.

Al-Anon and Adult Children of Alcoholics
New York: 800-245-4656
Outside New York: 800-334-2666

American Friends Service Committee
1501 Cherry Street
Philadelphia, PA 19102-1479
215-241-7169
A national and international Quaker organization "putting the power of love to work on behalf of those who need it most: the poor, the hungry, the hopeless victims of violence, discrimination, and injustice."

Association of Sexual Abuse Prevention
Professionals (ASAP)
Box 421
Kalamazoo, MI 49005
616-349-9072

Believe the Children
P.O. Box 1358
Manhattan Beach, CA. 90266
An organization for ritual abuse survivors and their caretakers.

Body-Healing Help
Elaine Westerlund, Ph.D.
Cambridge Women's Center
46 Pleasant St.
Cambridge, MA 02139

Center for Trauma and Dissociative Disorders
4400 E. Iliff Ave.
Denver, CO 80222-6087
800-441-6921 (outside Colorado)
303-759-6141 (Colorado)
Center for treatment of dissociative disorders, multiple personality disorder, ritual abuse, and post-traumatic stress.

Center on Sexual Abuse Pregnancy
International (CSAPI)
P.O. Box 82
Milton, VT 05468
800-639-1885

Changes
1721 Blunt Rd.
Pompano Beach, FL 33069
A magazine published by the U.S. Journal of Drug and Alcohol Dependence Inc., and Health Communications, Inc.

Healing Hearts
P.O. Box 6274
Albany, CA 94706
An organization for ritual abuse survivors and their caretakers.

Human Healing Arts, Inc.
Wendy Hoffman
P.O. Box 1898
New York, NY 10025
An organization for recovery and education through the performing and visual arts. Ritual abuse survivors are welcome.

Incest Awareness Project
Breaking The Silence (newsletter)
P.O. Box 8122
Fargo, ND 58109

I.S.A. (Incest Survivors Anonymous)
P.O. Box 5613
Long Beach, CA. 90804-0613
213-428-5599

Incest Resources, Inc.
For Crying Out Loud (newsletter)
Cambridge Women's Center
46 Pleasant St.
Cambridge, MA 02139
617-354-8807

Incest Survivor Information Exchange
Box 3399
New Haven, CT 06515
This organization produces a newsletter for adult survivors.

International Society for Study of Dissociative Disorders
5700 Old Orchard Rd.
Skokie, IL 60077
708-965-2776

Looking Up
P.O. Box K
Augusta, ME 04330
207-626-3402
Looking Up provides movement workshops, art exhibits, wilderness trips, and a newsletter entitles The Looking Up Times. *The organization also trains professionals.*

***MALE* Newsletter**
P.O. Box 460171
Aurora, Co 80046-0171
303-693-9930

Many Voices, *Words of Hope* (newsletter)
P.O. Box 2639
Cincinnati, OH 45201-2639
A newsletter for victims of trauma, dissociative patients, and post-traumatic stress victims. Subscription $30/year.

Model Mugging
P.O. Box 921
Monterey, CA 93942-0921
Teaches abuse victims to develop their physical self-defense skills.

National Center on Child Abuse & Neglect Clearinghouse
Department of Health and Human Services
P.O. Box 1182
Washington DC 20013
800-394-3366

National Council on Child Abuse & Family Violence
1155 Connecticut Avenue NW, Suite 300
Washington DC 20036
202-429-6695

National Resource Center on Child Sexual Abuse
63 Inverness Drive East
Englewood, CO 80112-5117
800-227-5242

Norma J. Morris Center for Healing from Child Abuse
2306 Taraval Street, Suite 102
San Francisco, CA 94116-2252
415-564-6002

Obsessive-Compulsive Disorder Foundation
P.O. Box 9573
New Haven, CT 06535
This group provides linkage for people with OCD and guidelines for support group development.

People for the American Way
2000 M St. NW #400
Washington, DC 20036
Arthur Kropp, president
202-467-4999
Publication: Attacks on the Freedom to Learn. *Also publishes papers, reports, and books. Nonpartisan constitutional liberties organization for business, media, and labor committed to reaffirming the traditional American values of pluralism, diversity, and freedom of expression in religion. PFAW was developed out of concern that an antidemocratic and divisive climate was being created by groups that sought to use religion and religious symbols for political purposes. Encourages Americans to maintain their belief in self.*

Phobia Society of America
P.O. Box 42514
Washington, DC 20015
This group publishes literature, research updates, resource directory, and self-help information.

PLEA Organization for non-offending males
356 W. Zia Rd.
Santa Fe, NM 87505
Men's groups that deal with victimization. Offenders not welcome.

Prevention and Treatment of Child Abuse & Neglect
1205 Oneida Street
Denver, CO 80220
303-321-3963

S.A.A. Sex Addicts Anonymous
Box 3038
Minneapolis, MN 55403

SAFE (Survivors of Abuse Find Empowerment)
114 Bergerville Road
Freehold, NJ 07728
908-462-4412

S.A.F.E. Home
P.O. Box 20677
Park West Finance Station
New York, NY 10025
A plan to develop a low-cost, grass-roots-therapy, place-of-respite, education project by survivors and professionals together.

SARA (Sexual Assault Recovery Anonymous)
P.O. Box 16
Surrey BC V3T 4W4 Canada

SCAP (Survivors of Child Abuse Program)
1345 El Centro Avenue
Box 630
Hollywood, CA 90028
800-422-4453

S.L.A.A. (Sex and Love Addicts Anonymous)
P.O. Box 119
New Town Branch
Boston, MA 02258
Offenders allowed.

Self-Help Clearing House
Attn: Sourcebook
St. Clares Riverside Medical Center
Danville, NJ 07834
212-642-2944
This group provides information on finding self-help groups and listings of local affiliates. A guidebook called The Self-Help Sourcebook *is available.*

S.I.A. (Survivors of Incest Anonymous, Inc.)
P.O. Box 21817
Baltimore, MD., 21222
410-282-3400
This organization lists Twelve Step support groups nationwide for incest and ritual abuse survivors.

SNAP (Survivors Network of Those Abused by Priests)
SNAP Newsletter
8025 South Honore
Chicago, IL 60620
312-483-1059

Society for Traumatic Stress Studies
P.O. Box 1564
Lancaster, PA 17603-1564
Organization for clinicians.

Survivorship
3181 Mission #139
San Francisco, CA 94110
This publication provides an international forum on torture, mind control, and ritual abuse.

The Cult Awareness Network
2421 W. Pratt Blvd.
Chicago, IL 60645
This network is for ritual abuse survivors and their caretakers.

The Healing Woman (magazine)
10895 Sutter Cir.
Sutter Creek, CA 95685
415-728-0339
A magazine for female incest survivors. Submissions accepted.

TRAANS (The Ritual Abuse Awareness Network Society)
P.O. Box 29064 Delamont Station
1996 W. Broadway
Vancouver, BC V6J 5C2 Canada
This group provides a newsletter, resources, and training.

Victimization and Self-Destructiveness
c/o Karen Conterio, Self-Injury Consultant
P.O. Box 267810
Chicago, IL 60626
Hart Grove Hospital Hotline 800-DONT-CUT

Voices Against Violence
c/o Patricia Kelly
TRS Suites
7 E. 30th Street
New York, NY 10016

V.O.I.C.E.S. (Victims of Incest Can Emerge Survivors)
IN ACTION, INC.
P.O. Box 148309
Chicago, IL 60614
312-327-1500
This group links people by mail and phone nationwide. It provides literature, conferences, local groups, and special interest groups (such as one for survivors who have experienced cult and ritual abuse).

Women For Sobriety (WFS)
Quakertown, PA 18951
215-536-8026 (24 hours)
Women only.

Bibliography

Barber, Paul. *Vampires, Burial, and Death: Folklore and Reality.* Binghamton, NY: Vail-Ballou Press, 1988.

Bartholomew. *I Come as a Brother: A Remembrance of Illusions.* Taos, NM: High Mesa Press, 1986.

Bateson, Gregory, and Mary Catherine Bateson. *Angels Fear: Towards an Epistemology of the Sacred.* New York: Macmillan Publishing Company, 1987.

Blume, Sue. *Secret Survivors: Uncovering Incest and Its Aftereffects in Women.* New York: Ballantine Books, 1991.

Booth, Leo. *When God Becomes a Drug.* Los Angeles: Tarcher, Inc., 1991.

Coles, Robert. *The Spiritual Life of Children.* Boston: Houghton Mifflin Company, 1990.

Conway, Flo, and Jim Siegelman. *Holy Terror: The Fundamentalist War on America's Freedoms in Religion, Politics, and Our Private Lives.* New York: Dell Publishing, 1982.

Dass, Ram, and Mirabai Bush. *Compassion in Action: Setting Out on the Path of Service.* New York: Bell Tower, 1992.

Deikman, Arthur. *The Wrong Way Home: Uncovering the Patterns of Cult Behavior in American Society.* Boston: Beacon Press, 1990.

Diamond, Sara. *Spiritual Warfare: The Politics of the Christian Right.* Boston: South End Press, 1989.

Fortune, Dion. *Psychic Self-Defense: A Study in Occult Pathology and Criminality.* Wellingborough, Northamptonshire: Aquarian Press, 1957.

Guggenbuhl-Craig, Adolf. *Power in the Helping Professions.* Dallas: Spring Publications, Inc., 1971.

Kornfield, Jack. *A Path with Heart: A Guide through the Perils and Promises of Spiritual Life.* New York: Bantam Books, 1993.

Kramer, Joel, and Diana Alstad. *The Guru Papers: Masks of Authoritarian Power.* Berkeley, CA: Frog Ltd., 1993.

Kubler-Ross, Elisabeth. *Death: The Final Stage of Growth.* London: Prentice-Hall, 1975.

Lamont, Stewart. *Religion Inc.: The Church of Scientology.* Great Britain: Harrap Ltd., 1986.

Larsen, Earnie. *Stage II Recovery: Life Beyond Addiction.* New York: Harper & Row, 1985.

Leedom, Tim. *The Book Your Church Doesn't Want You to Read.* Dubuque, IA: Kendall/Hunt Publishing Company, 1993.

Lewis, C.S. *Till We Have Faces.* New York: Harvest/HBJ, 1956.

Miller, Alice. *For Your Own Good.* Toronto: McGraw Hill Ryerson, Ltd., 1980.

Miller, Alice. *Thou Shalt Not Be Aware.* Toronto: Collins Publishers, 1984.

Miller, Alice. *The Drama of the Gifted Child: The Search for the True Self.* New York: Basic Books, Inc., 1981.

Reuther, Rosemary. *Religion and Sexism: Images of Women in Jewish and Christian Traditions.* New York: Simon & Schuster, 1974.

Rice, Anne. *The Vampire Chronicles.* New York: Random House, Inc., 1992.

Rutter, Peter. *Sex in the Forbidden Zone: When Men in Power—Therapists, Doctors, Clergy, Teachers, and Others—Betray Women's Trust.* Los Angeles: Tarcher, Inc., 1989.

Small, Jacquelyn. *Awakening in Time: The Journey from Co-Dependence to Co-Creation*. New York: Bantam Books, 1991.

Small, Jacquelyn. *Transformers: The Therapists of the Future*. Marina Del Ray, CA: DeVorss & Company Publishers, 1982.

Stone, Merlin. *When God Was a Woman*. Great Britain: Virago Ltd., 1976.

Trungpa, Chogyam. *Cutting through Spiritual Materialism*. Boston: Shambhala Publications, Inc., 1973.

Wilber, Ken. *The Holographic Paradigm and Other Paradoxes*. Boulder, CO: Shambhala Publications, Inc., 1982.

Wilber, Ken. *Grace and Grit: Spirituality and Healing in the Life and Death of Treya Killam Wilber*. Boston: Shambhala Publications, Inc., 1991.

Younger, Marlene. *Old Time Religion Is a Cult*. Palo Alto, CA: The Positive Attitude Press, 1985.

Zukav, Gary. *The Seat of the Soul*. New York: Simon & Schuster, 1989.

Glossary

Authoritarian: Someone in a leadership position who presents himself or herself as an unchallengeable authority.

Community: A group of two or more persons joined by common values and goals whose purpose it is to live in communion and harmony.

Chi: A Chinese word for what East Indians refer to as "prana." It is the universal energy, the basic essence and source of all life.

Chakras: A word from the Eastern traditions which means "rotating energy centers." There are seven primary chakras in the human body.

Cosmology: One's general theory of the cosmos or material universe, its parts, elements, and laws.

Devotee: One who is absorbed in devotion to or fervent admiration of another.

Devotion: A state of deep love for another in which our sense of self is the same as our sense of the person with whom we experience devotion.

Enlightenment: A state of illumination or awareness about who we truly are. An understanding of where the physical or material plane fits into the universal scheme of things.

Incarnation: The embodiment of spirit in flesh, as believed in the Eastern traditions.

Karma: Referred to in Eastern traditions as actions or deeds done by us that make up our destiny through the law of cause and effect.

Oneness: The state of "supreme identity as the one" or the awareness of no separation between things, beings, and events.

Psychospiritual perspective: The integration of our spiritual convictions and feelings with our mental thoughts and patterns.

Recovery: A returning to balance and a healing from compulsive and destructive behaviors. The first stage is retrieval of sobriety with food, drugs, alcohol, gambling, relationships, money, and others. Sobriety brings with it the ability to be in touch with and accept the world on its own terms. The second stage is the healing of our sense of separateness from God, the Goddess, All That Is, and other human beings. Recovery is the process of waking up to who we really are.

Ritual: Any act performed with conscious intention.

Sanyasin: Hindu word for "renunciate."

Separateness: The experience of existing in a state of disconnection from other people, places, things, and events. The opposite of the experience of oneness.

Service: A conscious (as opposed to a patterned or conditioned) response to another's need. Authentic service is done out of a spirit of recognition of the divine in the other and is performed out of our delight in serving the Self, of which we are all one.

Shadow: Aspects of ourselves that we don't see. Our shadow's sacred purpose is to reveal what we are resistant to seeing. A repressed shadow only grows bigger. Primitive cultures use ritual to manage their shadow side. When the shadow is acknowledged in ritual, it no longer governs us as it does when it is repressed. When we repress our shadow, others then have to carry it. This is an example of parasitic vampiring. Those of us who neglect our shadow are parasites.

Siddhis: Supernatural powers.

Social instinct: The natural inclination in each man or woman to seek interaction with others.

Soul: The aspect of human beings that is our essence. The soul remains intact no matter what happens to the body.

Spiritual abuse: The misuse of spiritual power. The act of using a position of power to take advantage of another. The betrayal of a trust. Preying on another's spiritual power for our own benefit.

Spiritual addiction: The obsessive search for the Self, or God, Goddess, All That Is, in someone or something *outside of ourselves*.

Spiritual autonomy: A state of confidence in ourselves through which we can trust ourselves, our intuition, our feelings, and our truth.

Spiritual incest: The forcing of physical presence, beliefs, or values onto another person by a person of authority in the name of God, religion, or spirituality. Can, but does not necessarily involve sexual energy.

Spiritual materialism: The compulsive or obsessive amassing or acquisition of spiritual accoutrements, techniques, or experiences with the belief that they are an indication of enlightenment.

Spiritual mirror: A spiritual teacher who, through his or her behavior, bodily gestures, and verbal confirmations, reflects back to students the truth that already lies within them.

Spiritual parasite: One who covertly "sucks" spiritual juice out of others in order to sustain his or her own sense of self-worth or enlivenment. The dysfunctional family is one example of a spiritual parasite in that its members arrange themselves around a dysfunctional authority figure and agree to a dance in which each member only gets to express one movement. The hero gets to achieve, the clown gets the laughs, the lost child gets acceptance, and the scapegoat gets to "act out" outrageousness.

Spiritual perpetrator: One whose nature it is to harm or diminish others' sense of self-empowerment through spiritual deception or abuse. For example, a spiritual teacher who uses his or her position to get sex, or a minister who regularly undermines the confidence of his or her parishioners with "Godly" criticism in order to get his or her way, foster dependency, or gain their worship.

Spiritual power: The life juice that animates human beings. The chi that is inherent in each of us by virtue of our being human. Our Godness, Goddessness, and goodness. Our life force.

Spiritual predator: One who preys on the chi or life juice of another for his or her own spiritual nourishment. The predator consciously seeks in very subtle and cunning ways the admiration and loyalty of others, thus gaining power and manipulation over those on whom he or she preys.

Spiritual seducibility: The attraction to spiritual teachers who foster dependency and perpetuate the illusion of separateness for their own profit or gain.

Spiritual vampirism: The act of draining others' energy by undermining their self-worth or stealing recognition that belongs to them. This leads to the destruction of the life juice of other human beings.

Toxic oneness: The seeking of great siddhis (supernatural powers) and "learning how to fly without learning how to land." Enhanced expression of the upper four chakras with weak expression of the lower three chakras. Not being grounded on the Earth. Also, an imbalanced focus on the state of oneness without an appropriate recognition of the many states.

Toxic service: Service done out of an attitude of pity or a feeling of "they need me." Or service rendered without recognition of the divine in the other.

Vedas: Holy Indian scriptures.

Index

absolute truth, 16
abuse, 16, 25, 45, 174, 218
abuse survivors, 20, 132, 180
addiction, 20, 37, 38, 74, 80, 93, 103, 108, 123, 145
adrenalin addiction, 37
adult rage, 45
African Shamanism, 75-76
agoraphobia, 132, 180
AIDS, 54, 93, 196
Ancient Wisdoms School, 75, 80, 163
Andrews, Lynn, 156
Aquarian Age, 16
archetype, 78
Asclepius, Greece, 186
ashram, 93, 210
atheist, 31
aura, 45, 144, 148
authoritarian, 78-79, 97, 124
authority, 16-17, 25, 32, 47, 59, 79, 94, 210
awakening, 74, 139, 207
awareness, 25, 74, 107, 160, 176, 223

Bali, 124-126, 216-220, 222
Banaras, 130
banjar, 220
Baptist, 194
bargaining phase, 180, 188, 190, 195
Berg, David, 173
Black, Claudia, 59
bliss, 26, 106, 145, 147, 148, 201, 208, 210
blood, 19, 30, 44, 47, 49, 61, 63, 69, 71, 82, 188
boundaries, 25, 33, 89, 169
Brahman, 130
Brennan, Barbara, 45
Buddha, 11
Buddhists, 31, 114
burning ghats, 130-131

Cardinal, 26
Catalys, 107
Catholic, 26, 54, 131
celibacy, 48
Celtic tradition, 76

chakra, 76, 146
charismatic, 49, 117, 142, 148
charlatans, 183
chi, 38, 45, 175, 217
chi-juice, 68, 89
Children of God, 173
Christian, 71, 76, 104, 114, 163
Christianity, 34, 76, 173
church, 27, 48, 69, 72, 104, 106, 108, 114, 174
cinderella complex, 82
co-creators, 11
codependency, 11, 81
collective awareness, 25
collective consciousness, 10, 155
community, 13, 17, 73, 80, 82, 125, 171, 186, 217, 219, 222
Compassion in Action, 243
compassion, 12, 29, 76, 128, 210
compulsive religiosity, 103, 104
consciousness, 14, 44, 75, 126, 127, 129, 145, 152, 163, 175, 177, 190, 200, 211, 214, 216
control, 25, 71, 87, 97, 100, 160, 161, 164, 168, 200, 216
coping behaviors, 24
cosmology, 33, 229
Cravens, Haddie, 143
Creative Leadership Training, 86, 88, 153, 155, 157
creativity, 25, 86, 87, 153, 155, 222, 229
creative visualization, 142, 153, 155, 159
crone, 88
cross, 131

dark side, 13, 128
Dass, Ram, 112, 124, 142, 145, 174-175
death, 48, 54, 104, 109, 115, 128, 138, 139, 176, 180, 191, 195
Deikman, Arthur, 78, 79
demons, 38, 124, 127, 212, 219
denial, 13, 15, 38, 60, 64, 74, 89, 92, 124, 154
dependency, 81, 82, 91, 133, 154, 187, 233
depression, 37, 45, 109, 155, 180, 215
devotee, 13, 208
devotion, 16, 209

251

disembodied beings, 112, 227
divine, 11, 17, 20, 83, 94, 125, 131, 166, 196, 217, 221
Dobrin, Dr. Richard, 45
dogma, 54, 85, 91, 123, 135
drug addict, 108
dry drunk, 152
dysfunctional family, 49, 59, 60, 64

earthquake, 170, 212, 214
eating disorders, 38
ego, 12, 47, 161, 163
Egyptian mysteries, 75, 76
Elaine, (survivor), 148, 151
Emmanuel, 112
empowerment, 15, 49, 99, 134, 173
energetic collar, 118
enlightenment, 11, 26, 59, 92, 97, 124
Epidaurus, 186
esoteric, 14, 75-76, 80, 163
essence, 45
EST, 160-163
evangelists, 24, 53
evolution, 18
existence, 14, 26, 76, 125, 131, 139
extrasensory, 76, 143, 153
extraterrestrial, 16

family dance, 49, 59, 64
family-of-origin, 17
Fassel, Diane, 151
faulty egos, 14
feminist, 165, 166
Fischer, Corey, 36
Fortune, Dion, 14, 23, 85, 243
fundamentalist, 19, 104, 114, 163, 190, 194, 243

Gangaji, 145-146, 176, 195, 199, 200, 205, 207, 210, 212, 222, 223
Ganges, 130, 207
gay, 193, 194, 196
genitals, 27
Gnosticism, 75, 76
God-image, 12
Goddess, 126, 248-249
Godness, 45, 194, 249
goodness, 45, 46, 249
grief, 35, 45, 79, 86, 93, 137, 180, 192-193, 205
groundedness, 20
guardian angels, 72, 175, 197
guru, 2, 12, 16, 56, 90, 92, 94, 98, 106, 129, 140, 148, 210, 233, 244

Hamlet, 187
Hands of Light, 45

harlots, 183
healing, 14, 20, 27, 74, 75, 90, 106, 114, 131, 152, 176, 186, 193, 219
heart attack, 7, 212-214
heterosexual, 195
heyoka, 197, 198
Hindi, 94, 214
Holy Brimstone, 51
holy person, 31, 45
hound of heaven, 24, 28, 177
human energy field, HEF, 45-47
hypervigilant, 53
hypnosis, 65, 104-105

I Ching, 91
immortal, 48, 123, 139
incarnation, 200, 223, 247
India, 7, 56-57, 92-94, 130, 208, 212, 214
inner worlds, 12
insanity, 74, 168, 181, 183-184, 188, 190
internal measuring stick of truth, 31

Jennings, Peter, 26
Jesus, 31, 32, 45, 46, 70, 163, 168, 174, 181, 222
Jesus Freak, 163
Joleen, (survivor), 116-124, 128
Jon, (survivor), 55-59
Jones, Jim, 54
Jung, Carl, 189

Kahuna, 75
karma, 148, 247
Katut, 218
kinesiology, 91
Koresh, David, 173
Kubler-Ross, Elizabeth, 180, 193

Larson, Earnie, 152
learning disabilities, 37, 66
Lewis, C.S., 187
life crisis, 6, 116
life force, 23, 45, 47, 53
Lifespring, 163
Living and Dying Project, 138, 193
log cabin theory, 189
lotus, 16
lovely death, 134, 138
Lucknow, 94, 131, 210
lust, 183

Mandela, Nelson, 213-214
manic-depressive, 77
martyr, 6, 142, 163
master, 16, 46, 199
mastery, 160
Medicine Woman, 156

medicine wheel, 197, 200
meditation, 19, 31, 106-107, 125, 143, 188, 206
mediums, 27, 187
metaphysics, 163
Michelle, (survivor), 190
millennium, 16
ministers, 19, 24, 34, 53, 173
missionaries, 32, 53
molestation, 27, 48, 88, 116
money changers, 31
Moon, Reverend, 142, 166
Mormon, 131, 132, 191, 192
myths, 48

NASA, 45
Native American, 36, 156, 163, 200
natural instincts, 23
Navajo, 75-76, 197
Nazarene, 23
near-death experience, 46, 113
New Age, 19, 74, 86, 124, 153, 206, 225
no mind, 26
Notre Dame, 26
Nyepi, 124, 127

occult, 76, 243
oneness, 26, 124, 145, 209
orgasm, 26, 120

Paine, Thomas, 25
paradise, 7, 216, 217, 220
paranoia, 180
parasite, 43, 48, 49, 52, 54, 55
parasitic, 43, 52, 54, 58, 60, 64, 68, 81, 96
parents, 12, 52, 79, 83, 142, 217, 218, 221
parenting, 11, 185
passion, 24, 28, 176, 177, 179, 216, 229
peak experience, 26
pedophile, 26
penis, 119, 122, 150
perennial wisdom, 75
perpetrator, 13, 18, 43, 49, 89, 96, 123
Perseid meteor showers, 138
personality, 15, 48, 94, 163
phases, 20, 106, 180, 189, 191, 193, 197
physical shock, 45
Pierrakos, Dr. John, 45
Piscean Age, 16
Poonjaji, 94, 103, 206-210, 212-215
Pope, 54
possession, 120
Power in the Blood, 69-70

power, 11, 14-15, 17-19, 28, 44, 46, 47, 49, 55, 68, 73, 76, 81, 82, 85, 104, 140, 141, 148, 160, 163, 165, 168, 172, 211, 225
prana, 45, 247
prayer, 31, 111, 125, 181, 214
preachers, 24
predator, 43, 49, 71, 77, 250
prey, 6, 67-68, 82, 87, 108, 141, 218
priest, 16, 65, 186, 225
protection, 17, 33, 79, 150
psyche, 13, 65
psychic, 29, 49, 76, 82, 144, 149, 156-158
psychic food chain, 49
psychic vacuum, 29
psychological law, 13
psychospiritual, 33, 109, 128, 188, 211

Rajneesh, 92-96
Ramana Maharshi, 59, 94, 139, 145, 176, 200, 211, 213-214
Randy, (survivor), 193-197
realization, 12, 16, 18, 205
recognition phase, 7, 180-181
reconciliation, 180
recovery, 81, 106, 142, 151-152, 195
reflection, 156, 199, 207, 210
rejuvenate, 127, 180, 221
religion, 16, 25, 125, 185
Rene, (survivor), 131-132, 191-192
repressed, 13, 48, 160, 184
reproduction, 23
resistance, 28, 124, 201
responsibility, 14-15, 155, 211, 221
revolutionary, 173, 199
Rex, (survivor), 89-92, 190-191
rheumatic fever, 181, 213
Rice, Anne, 244
right livelihood, 157, 176, 197
ritual abuse, 65, 132-133, 184
Ron, (survivor), 149-151
Rose, Betsy, 36, 39

sacred trust, 25
sainthood, 165
sanyasin, 94, 248
satsang, 200, 208, 210-211, 215, 222
scriptures, 24, 93
seduction, 6, 82, 103, 108, 123, 128-129, 139, 176
self-empowerment, 12
Self-expression, 16
self-preservation, 23
self-sacrificing, 164
service, 36, 57, 72, 133, 142, 148, 172-176, 222-223

service workers, 48
Sex and Love Addicts Anonymous, 194
sexual abuse, 13, 48, 73, 135, 142, 184
sexual molestation, 48, 88
sexuality, 25-26, 37, 48, 73, 76, 94, 184, 216, 222, 226
shadow, 13-15, 18, 233
shadow dance, 13
shadow side, 13, 233
shaman, 197
She's Flying, 203-204, 206, 212
silence, 36, 39, 94, 112-113, 125-127
Sioux, 23, 34-36, 199
sobriety, 151-152
social instinct, 23
soul, 49, 113-115, 117, 123, 131, 187, 196
species-type, 17
spirit, 28, 34, 110, 136, 140, 146, 170, 183, 196
spiritual abuse, 19-20, 25, 46-48, 64, 81, 103, 114, 179-181, 186, 188, 195
spiritual autonomy, 33
spiritual blood, 19, 44-45, 47, 49
spiritual high, 58
spiritual incest, 23, 25-28, 31-32, 36, 47-48, 73, 184
spiritual materialism, 142-145, 154
spiritual path, 13, 109
spiritual teachers, 13, 19, 43-44, 78, 129, 139, 142, 151, 204, 206, 209
spiritual vampires, 19-20, 29-30, 41, 43-45, 47, 96, 103, 114, 139-143, 148, 153, 188, 218, 222, 225
Stage II Recovery, 152
Steindl-Rast, David, 193
storytelling, 35, 186-187, 197
subconscious, 29, 48, 129, 156, 174, 190, 211
submission, 12
Sufism, 75
suicide, 98, 108, 113-114
supernatural, 32, 153
support system, 229
surrender, 75, 109, 124, 141, 152, 157, 177, 180, 191, 197, 200
surrender phase, 7, 180, 191, 197, 200
survivors, 20, 30, 132, 180, 188
susceptibility, 19, 44, 79, 103
syphon, 47
system of beliefs, 33, 89

temple, 31, 130-131, 219
The Naked Truth, 26
The Wrong Way Home, 78, 243
therapist, 49, 96, 127, 129, 132, 142, 167, 225, 231

Thich Nhat Hanh, 9, 171
Tibetan Book of the Dead, 114
Tibetan Buddhism, 75
Til We Have Faces, 187
Touch Institute, 219
toxic oneness, 124, 145
toxic service, 6, 142, 172, 174-175
toxic substance, 29
transcendence, 104
transformation, 34, 108, 151-153, 158, 175, 181, 183
transformational experiences, shifts, 30, 34, 184
transmission, 117, 146
trauma, 30, 61, 66, 77, 95, 104, 144, 159-160
Twelve Steps, 82, 194
Twelve Step sponsors, 19, 81, 82, 195, 225

unconscious aspects, 15
unconsciousness, 13, 14, 15, 16, 17, 49, 79, 96, 112, 123, 129, 175, 190, 248
unity consciousness, 145, 147
ungroundedness, 57, 154, 157

vagina, 120
Vaughn, (survivor), 187-188
Vedas, 93
victimhood, 13, 127
victims, 19, 44, 48-49, 194
visualizations, 142, 153, 154, 155
vision, 156, 157
Watts, Alan, 75
Whistling Elk, Agnes, 156
whole Self, 18
wholeness, 18-19, 60, 206
Wiccan, 163
withdrawal symptoms, 106, 132, 180, 204
Workaholics (WA), 37, 168
workshop leaders, 19
worship, 12, 233

XTC, 88

Yamuna, 208, 214
yoga, 108

About the Author

Marty Raphael has been sharing her insights into consciousness and spirituality in her life and in her work for over twelve years.

Born and raised near a Sioux Indian reservation in Montana, Marty is grateful to this day for the deep influence the Sioux people had on her as a youth. After studying psychology, religion, journalism and business in college, she went on to apply all of these disciplines in her business career. She has held executive positions in the medical manufacturing industry, trend-forecasting analysis firms and seminar companies.

Having spent approximately twenty years in the corporate arena, she is currently writing a second book about business as a spiritual path. In addition to maintaining a private prosperity consulting practice, Marty teaches storytelling to adults as a healing medium, plays piano and sings in her leisure. She has also studied formally with Sogyal Rinpoche and the Living and Dying Project where she facilitated the spiritual element of the dying process for terminally ill persons.

Her experience with spiritual abuse comes from a lifetime of spiritual searching which led to an intensive exploration of a variety of spiritual, psychological, and therapeutic healing modalities. She also conducted research into the use and misuse of spiritual power in diverse cultures such as India, Indonesia, Guatemala, and Mexico. Other formal research for *Spiritual Vampires* included leading workshops on healing from spiritual abuse, visiting ritual abuse survivors' groups, and interviewing dozens of teachers, gurus, ministers, therapists, and survivors of spiritual and ritual abuse.

ORDER FORM

Phone, fax or write if you would like a copy of our catalog listing all books, videos, etc. that we produce and distribute.

Telephone Orders: Call 505-474-0998 to charge your VISA, MasterCard, American Express or Discover
Fax Orders: 505-471-2584

Mail Orders: The Message Company
RR2 Box 307MM
Santa Fe, NM 87505

CODE	TITLE	QUANTITY	PRICE	TOTAL
D20063	**Spiritual Vampires:** The Use and Misuse of Spiritual Power	_____ x	$14.95 =	_____
D2008X	**Nikola Tesla's Earthquake Machine** 176 pages, 8½ x 11, paperback.	_____ x	$16.95 =	_____
D20101	**History of the American Constitutional or Common Law** 144 pages, 8½ x 11, paperback.	_____ x	$11.95 =	_____
D20039	**Universal Laws Never Before Revealed: Keely's Secrets** 288 pages, 8½ x 11, paperback.	_____ x	$19.95 =	_____
D20047	**Grazing Through the Woods with the Herb Man** Color video.	_____ x	$19.95 =	_____

SUBTOTAL _____

SHIPPING $2.00

NM RESIDENTS ADD SALES TAX 5.75% _____

TOTAL $ _____

❑ Enclosed is a check or money order for total.
❑ Please charge to my [ ] VISA [ ] MC [ ] American Express [ ] Discover

CARD #

EXP. DATE

SIGNATURE

NAME

ADDRESS

CITY / STATE / ZIP

PHONE